Advancing Christian Unity

SERIES EDITORS

Joel R. Beeke & Jay T. Collier

Interest in the Puritans continues to grow, but many people find the reading of these giants of the faith a bit unnerving. This series seeks to overcome that barrier by presenting Puritan books that are convenient in size and unintimidating in length. Each book is carefully edited with modern readers in mind, smoothing out difficult language of a bygone era while retaining the meaning of the original authors. Books for the series are thoughtfully selected to provide some of the best counsel on important subjects that people continue to wrestle with today.

Advancing
Christian Unity

Anthony Burgess

Edited by
Matthew Vogan

Reformation Heritage Books
Grand Rapids, Michigan

Advancing Christian Unity
© 2019 by Reformation Heritage Books

Reformation Heritage Books
3070 29th St. SE
Grand Rapids, MI 49512
616-977-0889
orders@heritagebooks.org
www.heritagebooks.org

Printed in the United States of America
22 23 24 25 26 27/10 9 8 7 6 5 4 3 2

Library of Congress Cataloging-in-Publication Data

Names: Burgess, Anthony, -1664, author. | Vogan, Matthew, editor.
Title: Advancing Christian unity / Anthony Burgess ; edited by
    Matthew Vogan.
Other titles: Sermons. Selections
Description: Grand Rapids, Michigan : Reformation Heritage Books,
    [2019] | Series: Puritan treasures for today | Summary: "An exposition
    of the topic of Christian unity in John 17"— Provided by publisher.
Identifiers: LCCN 2019027777 (print) | LCCN 2019027778 (ebook) |
    ISBN 9781601787125 (paperback) | ISBN 9781601787132 (epub)
Subjects: LCSH: Bible. John, XVII—Sermons—Early works to 1800. |
    Church—Unity—Sermons—Early works to 1800. | Sermons,
    English—17th century.
Classification: LCC BS2615.54 .B87 2019 (print) | LCC BS2615.54 (ebook)
    | DDC 252/.059—dc23
LC record available at https://lccn.loc.gov/2019027777
LC ebook record available at https://lccn.loc.gov/2019027778

For additional Reformed literature, request a free book list from Reformation Heritage Books at the above regular or e-mail address.

Table of Contents

Preface

Living in a Western culture that is ever polarizing in its values, ideas, and political views, we get used to division. The sheer multitude of diverse voices seems to promote the absence of unity. Divisive rhetoric is the norm in a cacophony of opinions. Christian values are frequently attacked with uncompromising hatred. Reconciliation and harmony seem both unthinkable and unattainable. The fault lines sometimes run so deep that they resemble a kind of civil war.

The church can also be a battleground of polarizing notions and methods. Certain trends in church organization and worship have become predominant and are at times dismissive of all else. Distancing ourselves from the wisdom of the past is commonly regarded as a virtue. Various doctrines that have been long regarded as inviolable are being reinterpreted or challenged. In responding to those views, believers may well assert and defend the truth, but the discernment to do so in love and with a genuine desire to gain others to the truth often lags behind.

This maelstrom of political, social, and ecclesiastical antagonism is not unlike the culture within which Anthony Burgess (d. 1664) ministered. His calling was to serve God in a generation that was literally experiencing civil war. During the civil war, royalist soldiers focused their fury on Puritan ministers, ransacking their houses and forcing them out. Along with thirty other Puritan ministers, Burgess took refuge in Coventry. He preached to the parliamentary garrison where there was a service every morning.

Burgess became involved in a project to unite the whole of the British Isles in the same doctrinal standards and church order. This was the result of the Solemn League and Covenant (1643), which bound the nations together in a religious, political, and military alliance. One vital and far-reaching result of that covenant was the Westminster Assembly. Its purpose was to discuss and affirm the key documents that would bind the nations ecclesiastically. Burgess preached before Parliament on six occasions, applying God's Word faithfully to that body and urging it to use its authority to help the work of Reformation.

During his time in London he engaged in the important defense of vital doctrines such as justification, original sin, and the moral law. Rejection of the moral law as a rule of life for believers was gathering momentum and was a key concern for the Westminster Assembly. Burgess was not only a sound teacher and formidable disputant; his sermons breathe the air of deep spiritual experience. He published more than a dozen volumes of careful biblical exposition and instruction. His most famous volume, *Spiritual Refining: The Anatomy of True and False Conversion*, has been called an "unequaled anatomy of experimental religion." Extending to more than a thousand pages, it covers many subjects of direct importance to the work of grace in the soul.

Burgess also preached 145 sermons on John chapter 17 alone.[1] He describes the whole prayer of Christ as a land flowing with milk and honey because of the abundant consolation it provides. The sermons were published in 1656, almost ten years after the Westminster Assembly had concluded its work. The ideal of uniting Christians and ministers seemed to have failed, in particular due to differences over questions of how the church should be governed. Yet we still draw inestimable benefit from the documents of the Westminster Assembly, especially the Confession of Faith and catechisms. They have been prized in the many parts of the world they

---

1. Anthony Burgess, *CXLV Expository Sermons upon the Whole 17th Chapter of the Gospel according to St John, or Christ's Prayer before His Passion Explicated and Both Practically and Polemically Improved* (London, 1656; forthcoming in 2 volumes in modern typeface by Reformation Heritage Books, 2019).

have reached. Burgess, for one, had not lost his desire for
unity; this is reflected in his exposition of Christ's prayer
for the unity of His people.

The following chapters include the sermons he
preached on the verses of John 17 that deal with unity,
here presented in a lightly edited and updated form.
The exposition emphasizes both the spiritual and visible unity that should exist within the church. Burgess
speaks of how union and communion with Christ
and His people are "the life and comfort of believers."
Careful consideration of the unity "which ought to be
amongst believers" introduces various other important
matters. Burgess deals especially with the means to preserve unity and the causes of divisions.

Burgess deals realistically and honestly with the
divisions that exist among Christ's people, as well as the
reasons for them. He does not accept that lack of unity
is inevitable but instead boldly calls it what it is according to Scripture: sin. We have become used to a cultural
context where the church is treated as a free-market
economy, where fresh start-ups arise and compete
against one another for a greater share of the market.
The church is often run and marketed using business
methodologies. Where this situation is accepted as posi-
tive, the question of unity is irrelevant unless it can be
used for competitive advantage.

There is also a tendency in our generation to belittle
the problem of outward divisions so long as there is a

degree of amicable association. Perhaps we are inclined to run to the opposite extreme from the Roman Catholic embrace of a false ecumenical movement by claiming that if true Christians are spiritually one in Christ, then visible unity is not important.

But if being spiritually one in Christ is all that matters, why do the Scriptures speak so often against division? Why indeed does the Lord Jesus Christ pray so earnestly for unity among His people in John 17 if being spiritually united is all that matters? There is a real unity of the church in its invisible or spiritual aspect. This is "the whole number of the elect, that have been, are, or shall be gathered into one, under Christ the Head thereof; and is the spouse, the body, the fulness of Him that filleth all in all" (Westminster Confession of Faith, 25.1). It is a number which no man can know and whose members are only ultimately known by God.

Yet the church is also manifested in this world in a visible way—in its order and government, for instance. According to the Westminster Confession of Faith, the visible church "consists of all those throughout the world that profess the true religion; and of their children: and is the kingdom of the Lord Jesus Christ, the house and family of God." Christ has entrusted it with "the ministry, oracles, and ordinances of God, for the gathering and perfecting of the saints, in this life, to the end of the world" (25.3–4).

The visible church involves visible office-bearers

administering the visible ordinances appointed by Christ to those who have a visible profession of the true religion, as distinguished from the rest of the world. It is the means used to gather the invisible church. When Scripture uses the word for church, it may refer to the visible aspect, the invisible aspect, or to both (although one of them is usually foremost). The context in which the word is found makes the interpretation clear. For instance, Paul speaks of having "persecuted the church of God, and wasted it" (Gal. 1:13; cf. Acts 8:3). This is evidently the visible church, since the invisible church cannot be wasted or persecuted.

Although in our own day many people have little time for the unity of the church and do not worry about questions of schism, unity and division remain vitally important matters. The spectacle of competing denominations has become a fact of life to many, rather than a scandal. They shun the kind of hyper-separatism that regards any unity as conspiracy by publicized common causes based on a generalized minimalist set of convictions.

Yet, if a minimalist set of relations between denominations can exist while denominations remain separate, there is an implicit statement that the visible unity of the church is either not real or not important and that the reasons for separation do not matter. Too many of us "are not grieved for the affliction of Joseph" (Amos 6:6). There seem to be very few saying, "My brethren, these things ought not so to be" (James 3:10). The Puritan Samuel Hudson writes, "Division is the Devil's music, but that which makes the Devil laugh should make us cry."

The goal and aim of the Westminster Assembly was very different. It contrasts markedly with the indifference to unity often displayed by those who aim to stand within the Puritan and Reformed tradition today. As James Walker records, the Congregationalists at the Westminster Assembly proposed a friendly coexistence and occasional communion with the Presbyterians which, while separate in government, would, they claimed, be "no plain and total separation, we shall be working substantially towards the same end." This was resolutely declined with the following explanation:

> So might the Donatists and Novatians have pled, and indeed almost all the separatists who have figured in the Church's history. Such separation was unknown in the apostles' time, unless it were used by false teachers: all who professed Christianity then held communion together as one Church. If you can join with us occasionally in acts of worship, you ought to act with us in joint communion, not in separated congregations. God's way of revealing truth to such as are otherwise minded, is not by setting men at a distance from each other. That you should be a distinct Christian organization, taking members from our

Churches who may have scruples of conscience, is schism undoubted in the body of Christ.

The Westminster divines were therefore opposed to the now popular notion that church differences and competing distinctions are a good thing, and diversity is strength. They considered carefully the New Testament's firm emphasis on uniformity (1 Cor. 11:1, 16; 14:29, 33–35, 40; 16:1–2), as it exhorts us to "walk by the same rule" (Phil. 3:16) and to "stand fast in one spirit, with one mind striving together for the faith of the gospel" (Phil. 1:27). "I will give them one heart, and one way, that they may fear me" (Jer. 32:39).

The Scottish theologians who were contemporaries of the English Puritans worked through these issues carefully. They sought to understand and apply the scriptural teaching on unity and schism with accuracy. Men like James Durham stressed that unity was an absolute priority and duty, and that schism was a serious sin. Yet they acknowledged that separation is sometimes a duty where sinning is the price of maintaining unity. Such questions may be vexed and complex to work through in practice, but there must always be love for the unity of the church and genuine grief when it cannot be attained.

It is important to understand this background in order to appreciate the principles undergirding what Anthony Burgess says on the subject. Burgess gives practical counsel in this area in demonstrating the spirit that

Christians ought to have toward one another. He will not allow us simply to show regret and concern while doing nothing about the divisions of the church. We are under the strongest obligations not only to "pray for the peace of Jerusalem" (Ps. 122:6) but also to be peacemakers. Blessed are the peacemakers who join their prayers with that of the great Head of the church: "That they all may be one" (John 17:21).

—Matthew Vogan

CHAPTER 1

The Blessing of Unity among Ministers

Christ prays "that they may be one, as we are" (John 17:11). Some say that this relates to the way in which God keeps the disciples, as if it specifies the thing that would keep them. If they agree in love among themselves, they are sure to be preserved. We understand this instead as a distinct blessing. As Christ prayed for the disciples to have sound faith before, so now He prays for their union and love.

We may consider the disciples in a twofold way: first, as *believers and disciples*, along with others, given by God to Christ. The unity of believers among themselves in this way is a precious blessing. Second, as *preachers*. They may be considered as men in office, as those who were appointed to preach the gospel, and so our Savior prays for their unity in relation to this.

It is of infinite consequence that the ministers of the gospel should agree among themselves, for when ministers are divided the people must be divided. If the pilots in a ship disagree, the ship must necessarily sink. Knowing the devices of Satan to set apostle against apostle and pastor against pastor, our Savior therefore prays for unity among ministers in their ministerial office and employment.

It is a remarkable expression. He does not pray that they may be united, but that they may "be one," and that they may "be one" according to the highest example of all unity, the Father and the Son. Luther thinks that being "one" refers to one spiritual body, but we rather take it as their office and ministerial employment. The apostle, arguing against church divisions because of one minister being thought superior to another, says, "he that planteth and he that watereth are one" (1 Cor. 3:8). They all have the same objective and all have one general employment: the conversion of souls to God.

Unity among Ministers Is a Special Blessing

It is a special blessing when the ministers of the gospel agree as one. Nothing is so terrible to the church's adversaries as the unity of pastors. This was the reason (some say) why our Savior chose apostles who were mostly related to each other. It was so that their love would be preserved more inviolably. Our Savior also gave the disciples this counsel: "Have salt in yourselves, and have peace one with another" (Mark 9:50). "Have salt," that is, season the world and one another with grace. But lest this salt would sting and smart too much, He adds, "and have peace one with another." Peace and love are of such great concern that He leaves peace with them as a legacy: "Peace I leave with you, my peace I give unto you" (John 14:27). He gives them a "new commandment"—to love one another (John 13:34). Indeed, He makes this a sign of their discipleship—not if they cast out devils or work miracles, but if they love one another.

What Unity Should Ministers Have?
1. Unity of Faith
They should believe the same doctrine, which is therefore called "one faith" (Eph. 4:5). There is no other foundation but one, the Lord Christ (1 Cor. 3:11). This must be the foundation of all other unity. Although Roman Catholics make unity a mark of the true church, we say that unity without true doctrine is a mere faction, a conspiracy. Muslims have unity, Jews have unity, but because they do not have the true doctrine, it is not true peace and concord. True doctrine is the soul, the fountain, and the root of all.

2. Unity of Confession
A second unity is found in the same confession and acknowledgment of faith. This should be in the same words. It is very desirable not only to hold the same doctrinal points but to use the same words also. New words bring in new doctrines. Thus, the apostle, in pressing

unity, exhorts them not only to be "in the same mind and in the same judgment" but to "speak the same thing" (1 Cor. 1:10). Timothy is exhorted to "hold fast the form of sound words" (2 Tim. 1:13). Even though they were only words and a form, yet he must hold them fast. This made the early church so tenacious about the Greek word for "same substance" (to refer to Father, Son, and Spirit), because by that word all heretical opinions about the Trinity (such as those stemming from the Greek word for "similar substance") were excluded.

It is a remarkable expression that God is said to speak "by the mouth of his holy prophets" (Luke 1:70). Although there were many prophets, it says "mouth," not "mouths," as if they all had but one mouth, and spoke the same thing. There ought, therefore, to be only one mouth for all the ministers of the gospel in confessing what they believe. We should be able to know what all teach by what one teaches.

3. Unity of Affection

There must be unity of affection and hearts. When the church first began to increase, their unity of affection was greatly commended. They "continued with one accord" (Acts 1:14; see also Acts 2:1, 46). "The multitude of them that believed were of one heart and of one soul" (Acts 4:32). Though they were a multitude, they had only one heart and soul.

Why Is Unity among Ministers a Great Blessing?

1. Unity Strengthens the Church

Fortitude and strength are found in unity. Strength united is stronger. "Every kingdom divided against itself is brought to desolation," our Savior says (Matt. 12:25). When one piece of the wall divides from the other, it foretells ruin. In Aesop's fable, a father gave a bundle of sticks to his sons to show them that while the pieces were together it was impossible to snap them, but taken one by one they were easily broken. By this he taught them that as long as they agreed they were invincible. All the united power of the church is little enough against their common enemies, so why would they want to weaken themselves?

2. Unity Defends the Church

Unity among ministers not only strengthens, it also opposes the Enemy (the devil and all he uses) with greater success. Roman Catholic opponents reproach us with the number of different Protestant sects that exist. Although we can retort by reminding them of their own divisions even in fundamental matters, it is still our shame and grief that such a charge is even in some measure true. It may not be true to the extent that our opponents allege, since none of the Reformed differ in fundamental matters. We do not accept as Reformed those who deny fundamental matters such as Christ's deity and substitutionary atonement. Yet differences among the Reformed certainly give an advantage to Roman Catholics which they can use with those who are unsettled. "Look," they say, "they have no certainty among themselves; they do not know where to stop. The Lutheran judges the Calvinist diabolical." Unstable and unthinking individuals regard this as a great argument against the truth.

Yet even in the times of the apostles the church of God had sad divisions (1 Cor. 3). Let us bewail the corruption of the best, that they should be carried away with bitterness so far as to neglect the truths of God by giving advantage to the common Enemy.

3. Unity Prevents Division

Unity is of great consequence among the ministers of the gospel because their divisions breed divisions among the people. Differences among teachers breed irreconcilable agitations among the people. We see in the church of Corinth, when the teachers were divided, what sort of divisions there were among the people when some were for Paul and some for Apollos.

4. Unity Edifies Souls

We should pray to God for unity among ministers because their disputes bring neglect of the chief work of their ministry. This is to build up souls in their way to heaven. This is the purpose for which God has called us to be ministers. When those of us who are ministers fall out with one another and set up opinion against opinion, the work of the ministry is greatly retarded. Thus the apostle urges Timothy to flee from unprofitable disputes and quarreling (2 Tim. 2:14, 23). This is because they eat away at godliness. They are like thorns and nettles among the corn, hindering its growth.

5. Unity Is Consistent with God and His Gospel

Unity among ministers is to be desired because it agrees with their office and call. They preach the gospel of peace, God is the God of peace (Col. 3:15), Christ is the Prince of Peace, and He is our peace reconciling all things. Why then should the minister's tongue be a tongue of war, as if they were priests to Bellona, the Roman goddess of war, rather than ministers of the gospel?

If all these principles are considered, we may well pray with our Savior, "Lord, make the ministers of the gospel as one man. For divisions," as Jerome said, "are the loss of friends, the gain of enemies, and the public kindling of God's anger."

Why Do Ministers Disagree?

What are the reasons (you may ask) that make the ministers of the gospel disagree in this way?

Sin

In general, it is due to the corruption and sin which lurks in the hearts of all, so that it is more to be wished for than expected to have Jerusalem a city compactly built within itself. Never expect in this world to see a time in which all the ministers of the gospel will have one faith, one heart, and one mouth. This is reserved for heaven, where there will be no difference between Calvinists and Lutherans, between various forms of church government. The church of God has always been on fire, and as when a house is on fire, some call for water, some for ladders, some to pull down the house, so some have cried for more moderate means and some for extreme and vehement means.

Self

Ministers can disagree due to corrupt affections such as pride, ambition, and covetousness. The apostles charge these things against the false teachers. Diotrephes loved to have preeminence (3 John 1:9). Others counted gain to be godliness; their hearts were exercised with covetous practices. No heretic who ever proved to be a firebrand in the church was not mostly moved by one of these causes. Augustine added to the definition of a heretic that it was for some temporal advantage that they invented or propagated their false opinions.

Satan

Even the best of ministers have corruption in them and Satan is ready to blow on any sparks immediately to start a fire. There have been contentions and differences among the most eminent pillars in the church. We read of the disciples contending among themselves twice concerning having supremacy over one another. Scripture tells us of a sharp controversy between Paul and Barnabas (Acts 15). Paul and Peter had a hot contest in relation to an area of religious practice. If the sun and moon collide in this way, an eclipse in the church is inevitable. And who can speak also with a tender enough heart of the many oppositions and divisions between Calvinists and Lutherans, and others of the Reformed church?

All of this makes us see the necessity of Christ's prayer for unity. There is such corruption in our hearts and Satan is so busy making differences and disputes, that although legions of devils can agree to be in one man, yet Satan will not allow two teachers to agree in one church.

Application

Follow Christ in this prayer. Give the great God of heaven no rest by prayer till He has given rest to His church and its guides. Cry out to Christ, as the disciples did, to rebuke the winds and tempests, for the ship we are in is sinking. These divisions are not only sins but also sad omens of God's wrath, as if He intended to unchurch us and make us no more His people, as He did to the churches in Asia.

CHAPTER 2

The Pattern for Unity among Ministers

We now come to the example or pattern of the unity which Christ prays for. "That they may be one, as we are" (John 17:11). He does not pray for every kind of unity. He wants them to imitate the most absolute and complete unity: the unity of the Father and the Son.

The Unity of the Father and Son
1. Unity of Agreement
Some say that this unity between the Father and the Son cannot mean unity of being, but rather a unity of agreement. It is compared to the unity of believers, which is a unity of agreement rather than a unity of essence. Yet even if it is a unity of consent in will and agreement (as Calvin interprets it), it does not follow that other places speaking of their oneness should also be understood in the same manner. In fact, from the oneness of will between the Father and Son the oneness

of their nature is necessarily inferred. Even if we understand this as principally meaning unity in will, yet by consequence it would prove to mean unity of nature, for in free agents, where there is the same will, there is also the same nature. Where there is the same human will, there is the same human nature, and where there is the same divine will, there is the same divine nature. Of course with men it is the same specific nature, not the same numerical nature. But because there is only one God, therefore it must be the same numerical nature.

2. Unity of Essence

We are to take the unity of the Father and the Son referred to here in as large a sense as it appears in other passages (or at least not to exclude it). In other passages, especially John 10:30, "I and my Father are one," we have undeniable arguments to prove that it is a unity of essence. Bellarmine (though a Roman Catholic) uses three arguments.

First, there must be unity of essence between the Father and the Son because otherwise our Savior's argument would be insufficient. Christ argues, "None can pluck my sheep out of my hands, because none can pluck them out of my Father's hands." Why does this follow? Because "I and my Father are one." If Christ and the Father did not have one power, and so one divine nature, the argument would not hold.

A second reason why there must be unity of essence is because the Jews understood him in this sense, and therefore they took up stones to stone him. Mark the reason: "Because that thou, being a man, makest thyself God" (John 10:33). If our Savior had meant no more than unity of agreement with God's will, the Jews knew that every godly man had the love of God in this sense written in his heart. They could not think that that claim was blasphemy. They did not think that David made himself God, when he delighted in the law of God, making his will to accord with God's.

Thirdly, there must be unity of essence because our Savior on this accusation does not deny what He is accused of, nor does He charge them with falsehood. Instead He further proves it. Because He does the works of the Father, therefore He bids them believe His works, if they will not believe Him, which are to make them know that the Father is in Him, and He in the Father. Upon these words it is said again, "They sought again to take him" (John 10:39), implying that He had not corrected but further confirmed what they called blasphemy.

3. Unity of Equality

In the third place, though our Savior prays that the disciples may be one, as He and the Father are, yet their argument will not hold unless they can show that the word "as" is always used as a note of equality, and not similitude only. But we can show the contrary in Scripture, that "as" is used here for similarity, not equality. For example, "Be ye therefore merciful, as your Father also is merciful" (Luke 6:36). There, it is a note of similarity only, for how can a drop be equal to the ocean? Similarly, "Every man that hath this hope in him purifieth himself, even as he [God] is pure" (1 John 3:3). Here it must be a note of similarity, for no one can be equal to God in purity.

This is also found in our text: "That they may be one, as we are" (John 17:11). This does not mean that you can equalize their unity, but rather that you can propound it as the absolute and perfect rule to follow. If you consider this text, it eliminates the Arian view (that Christ is a created being distinct from and subordinate to the Father), and so is a testimony of the faith, which they perverted into a reason for treachery. Augustine observes that Christ prays, "that they may be one, as we are." He does not say, "that they may be one *with us*," or "that *they and we* may be one, as we are one," but "that they may be one, as we are one." We will say more about this when we come to verse 21.

Ministers Must Strive for the Most Perfect Unity, That of the Father and Son

It is not enough for the ministers of the gospel to be one. They are to strive for the most perfect unity, to be one as the Father and Son are one. It should make us blush and be ashamed to see the contentions and differences that exist between ministers. Did the Father and Son ever show such discord? We should never take our eyes off this pattern. Let us consider how many ways we are to aim for the unity that exists between the Father and Son.

1. A Spiritual Unity

First, the unity between the Father and the Son is a spiritual unity. Some have called the Spirit of God the holy bond of the Trinity—and His is not a physical, bodily unity, but a spiritual unity. So must the ministers of the gospel be. Though they are of the same nature, of the same flesh and blood, yet if they do not have the same spirit composing and sanctifying them, they will be like ropes of sand. This the apostle urges admirably, where, when enumerating the various gifts and operations of God's Spirit, he still adds, it is "the same Spirit" (1 Cor. 12:4), and "by one Spirit we are all baptized into one body" (1 Cor. 12:13).

This then ought to be our unity. The Holy Spirit of God is to move, work, and guide all our hearts and affections, as it is the same soul that informs all the parts of the body, or as (to put it the way some philosophers have said) there is one "active intellect" which is universal to all men.[1] There may be agreement for civil and political considerations, but this will never hold till there is a spiritual

---

1. Here Burgess means the faculty that makes potential knowledge into active knowledge.

unity. As Cicero observed, all friendship founded on convenience, or pleasure, would never endure unless virtue were added to the relationship. We may add further that even virtuous and moral good is not ground enough for unity, unless it is a spiritual good. If the Spirit of God worked the same measure of illumination and sanctification in everyone, there would not be any disagreement, but though all the godly have the same Spirit, yet they do not have the same gifts or graces, or degree of graces. And for lack of this comes contention.

2. A Constant Unity

Secondly, the unity between Father and Son is constant and undivided. There can never be a separation between them. The Father and the Son were always one, though the manifestation of this is greater under the gospel light than it was under the law.

Thus, the ministers of the gospel ought to agree constantly and perpetually. For, if at any time contention breaks forth, it proves to be like a dead fly in a box of ointment. It makes all the other good they have to be spoken of poorly. No matter how learned, how godly, how zealous they are, discord will scandalize everyone.

This constancy of unity is to be preserved against all outward or inward causes of difference. Outward difference is caused by the persecution and opposition of enemies to the church of God. Inward difference comes from our own corruptions and distempers. Against both we are to watch, so that our peace will not be weakened.

3. A Holy Unity

Thirdly, the unity of the Father and the Son is a holy unity. They are one in what is holy and heavenly. They only will what is good. The sun may sooner become a dunghill than they would will what is evil. Let the ministers of God strive for such a unity. Unity in error, unity in sin and wickedness, is the sort of unity the devils have among themselves. The unity among Roman Catholics, which they boast of, is it not like the unity of Herod and Pilate, both agreeing against Christ?

4. A Philanthropic Unity

Fourthly, the unity of the Father and the Son is full of love to mankind. They both are one in this, to procure the salvation of believers. The Father wills to send His only begotten Son, to die that reproachful death, and to be an atonement for man's sins. The Son voluntarily and readily undertakes this bitter cup. They are one to procure the salvation of man. If the Father and the Son had disagreed, no salvation would have been possible.

Oh then that the ministers of the gospel would make this use of their unity, that they would all as one man endeavor for the conversion and edification of souls! How happy would it be to lay all differences and disputes aside, so that they would bring people to the saving knowledge of God! What a spur this should be to us! Does the Father not think His Son too dear? Does the Son not think His blood too dear for men's souls, and shall we ruin souls by contentions? Do we not then take on the devil's work, and not Christ's?

5. A Well-Ordered Unity

Fifthly, the unity of Father and Son is a well-ordered unity. Though there is a unity of nature, yet this does not breed a confusion of the persons: the Father is the Father, and the Son is the Son. For all this unity, they are not one person, though they are one essence or substance.

Thus the unity among God's ministers, and among the people, must not degenerate into confusion. The difference between shepherd and sheep, between governors and governed in the church, must be maintained. When the devil cannot divide, he aims to bring unity into confusion, by inducing people to give up the differences between their gifts and offices. As Korah and his company told Aaron, "Ye take too much upon you, seeing all the congregation are holy, every one of them" (Num. 16:3), implying that there was no difference between the congregation of Israelites and the priesthood.

In 1 Corinthians, the apostle Paul urges unity fervently, and he does so because we are one body, yet he shows that there is a difference between the members in the body. Every member is not the eye; so neither is every one a preacher, an officer in the church. This false kind of unity ends in all schism and disorder at last.

6. A Perfect, Absolute Unity

Lastly, the unity of the Father and the Son is most perfect and absolute. It is an essential unity. Although we cannot have this unity, yet this should teach us to aim at the highest degree of unity we can. We are not to allow the least grudging and complaining or the least proud or envious thoughts against one another. We are to love one another more than father or children, than husband or wife, or any kind of relation that has a unity based on flesh; this prayer of Christ calls for a higher unity, "that they may be one, as we are."

How to Get and Keep This Unity

We have heard about the duty and necessity of unity, as well as the causes that break it, and what good remedies may be prescribed to keep this excellent harmony. Although I shall not launch into this whole point, deferring it till John 17:21, yet I shall briefly remind you of some ways of keeping unity.

1. Pray for Peace

First, we are earnestly to pray to God to bestow such a spirit of concord. It is not the industriousness or policy of all the conciliators, moderators, and pacificators in the world that can bring this about, but God only can bend men's hearts for it. Hence we see our Savior praying to the Father for this agreement, and God is called the God of peace because He only can make peace in the church and state. When an evil contentious spirit is among the prophets, as well as when God sends a lying spirit among them, it is from God's anger and wrath. When the temple was to be destroyed, the rending of it was an omen of its desolation. When God is going to unchurch a church, and make a garden a wilderness, divisions are commonly the antecedent causes of it.

2. Be Sympathetic with Each Other

A second rule is to rejoice in the abilities and gifts of others and the success accompanying them, as much as if they were our own when God is glorified by them. We should also be compassionately affected by the weaknesses and failings of others.

These two are necessarily joined together, and they are able to cement and unite all differences. When John's disciples came with an envious spirit against Christ, and said, "All men come to him" (John 3:26), this would have been enough to leaven and sour John's heart. But see his excellent spirit, "He must increase, but I must decrease" (John 3:30). He was willing that Christ's light and glory should be exalted, though it darkened and obscured his. This is a good reconciler.

We should also show a tender forbearing of one another, bear with one another's weaknesses, and be prone to forgive the rashness of others. If the stones of Jerusalem were thus polished and smoothed, they would lie even and firm together.

3. Love the Church's Well-Being

A third rule is, love the public good of the church. If this reigned in our hearts, it would resolve all differences. The true mother's love would not permit her to have the child divided in two. It must be selfish revenge that makes two enemies desire to see the ship they are in sink rather than agree to preserve it. It was great self-denial in Jonah to give himself up to destruction rather than have the whole ship endangered. Everyone ought to say, "If I am the Jonah, cast me out." The Romans had a dedicated temple called Jupiter's depository, because there they would go and deposit or lay aside their mutual contentions before they entered into the Senate house. What a shame it is when many heathens have laid aside their mutual quarrels for the common good, yet Christians fail to! Shall not the ministers of the gospel do much more than the heathens for the church's safety?

4. Be Fair

A fourth rule: do not accuse people of holding consequences from their doctrine that are not inevitable consequences from their views, and consequences which they in fact abhor. In doctrinal disputes this is oil to the flame. Lutherans take the Calvinist doctrines about predestination and accuse Calvinists of teaching that God is the author of sin, cruel and unjust, worse than Pharaoh, who commanded brick but gave no straw, and even cruel like Nero, who having a mind to put a vestal virgin to death, caused her to be ravished, and then put her to death because she was ravished. But the Calvinists detest and abhor all such consequences, and if they recognized that such conclusions followed necessarily from their doctrines, they would publicly abjure them. Some gathered from Paul's preaching of free grace that, therefore, men might sin that grace might abound. But against this Paul cries, "God forbid!" (Rom. 6:2) and says that the damnation of such logicians is just (Rom. 3:8).

5. *Build on Existing Unity*

Lastly, so far as people agree with us in the fundamentals, let them retain peace and concord. The apostle exhorts, "Whereto we have already attained, let us walk by the same rule" (Phil. 3:16). It is God's mercy that the Reformed churches, though differing in many opinions, yet do not dissent in fundamentals. (I do not reckon Socinians among the Reformed, and indeed some do not even include them among Christians because they deny the deity of Christ.) But the Reformed in general keep the same foundation, though some are purer churches than others. Now it is a special preservative of charity to embrace one another with hearty affections. To that extent, therefore, it is an uncharitable and peevish thing in some Lutherans that they will not call Calvinists brethren or allow reconciliation, but profess that they would rather reconcile with the pope, whom they maintain to be antichrist.

Application

Run to the God of peace to settle peace and truth. The greater the mercy is, and the more the devil opposes it, the more you should strive for it. How many unities does the apostle mention in Ephesians 4? And why then should we be many? "Blessed are the peacemakers: for they shall be called the children of God" (Matt. 5:9).

CHAPTER 3

The Nature of Christian Unity

"That they all may be one; as thou, Father, art in me, and I in thee" (John 17:21). The chief matter of Christ's petition is laid down in this verse. What is it that He prays for on behalf of those who shall believe in Him? It is *unity* and *agreement* among themselves. As He prayed for the apostles before that they "might be one" as apostles in the work of the ministry, so here He prays for all believers.

It is such a great matter to have all the godly in union among themselves. This union includes grace begun here and glory consummated hereafter. It must be considered again and again that these glorious privileges are to be included in their union. It is as though everything is preserved if this is preserved, and without that there could not be any godliness here or blessedness hereafter. The *unity* and *agreement* of all believers is the principal part of Christ's petition for them. Take notice of the following in relation to that reality:

1. The *benefit itself*. It is "that they all may be one."

2. The *universal extent of this unity*. "That they all." Though there is great variety and difference in gifts, in graces, in offices, in outward condition, yet they must all be one.

3. The *pattern of this unity*. "As thou, Father, art in me, and I in thee."

4. The *nature and quality* of this unity. "That they also may be one in us."

5. The *fruit* of this unity. "That the world may believe thou hast sent me."

I shall first consider the benefit prayed for: "that they all may be one." That union among the godly is of so great a necessity and consequence that Christ principally and chiefly prays for this on their behalf. He does not say that they may love and agree with one another but that they may "be one." It is as if the church is but one person and, as the apostle argues, "No man ever yet hated his own flesh" (Eph. 5:29). So there should be no divisions, envy, and differences among the godly, because they are one spirit, as it were. They should no more hate one another than a man hates himself. Though grace and sanctification are included in this unity, yet that which is expressly mentioned is their agreement. From this text I shall pursue *union among believers*. Consider that there is a twofold unity among the godly. And because our Savior enlarges upon it Himself, I shall also insist upon it.

To open up this truth, consider that there is a twofold unity or union among the godly: invisible and visible.

Invisible Unity

Invisible unity is that by which, being united to Christ their Head by the Spirit on God's part, and faith on our part, they receive spiritual life and increase. In this respect, believers are compared to the several members of the body and Christ is compared to the head because of that spiritual life and motion they receive from Him. This is the foundation of our visible union, and without this, though we may be part of the church outwardly, yet indeed we receive no saving advantage by Christ. The text does not speak of this union because it is such a union that the world, in seeing it, may be induced to believe.

Visible Unity

There is therefore a visible union by which believers outwardly and visibly express their compacted nearness to one another. And so those particular churches of Corinth and Ephesus are called Christ's body in respect of their external as well as their internal union. For we have fellowship with Christ and with one another not only by faith but also by the ordinances.

The text speaks of this visible unity and this is made a special means to bring the world to believe. Whereas on the contrary, differences of opinion and sad rents and sects in religion are the only way to confirm men in their impiety, and to think there is no truth and no religion at all. This visible union diffuses itself in many branches.

Unity of Faith and Profession

Believing and speaking the same thing must be laid as the foundation of unity; for unity in error, idolatry, or false ways is not peace but a faction or conspiracy. This unity of faith is reckoned among the many unities the apostle mentions in Ephesians 4:5 and Philippians 2:2. Believers are exhorted to be "of one mind," and the apostle notably urges this: "that ye all speak the same thing," being "perfectly joined together in the same mind and in the same judgment" (1 Cor. 1:10). What a sad breach then the devil has made upon God's people when there are so few of the same mind who judge the same things.

But (as was said above) there must be a sameness and unity in the true faith. For the Jews are one among themselves, the Muslims are one, and the Roman Catholics are one in such a way that they boast of it and make it a sign of the true church. Now, even if this should be granted (though they have a thousand divisions among themselves), it is still nothing at all unless it is unity in the faith and in sound doctrine.

Unity of Affection and Love in the Heart and Outwardly toward One Another

Love is called the affection of union and it makes a man to be the object of love as much as he loves the object.

And we see the prayer of Christ abundantly fulfilled in this respect concerning the first Christians, for it is said that they "were of one heart and of one soul" (Acts 4:32). Those thousands of believers were as if they had but one heart and soul among them. Thus, in Tertullian's time, the heathen admired the love Christians had for one another. Our Savior makes it a surer sign of discipleship than if they wrought miracles (John 13:35).

Unity in the Ordinances of Public Worship God Has Appointed

As God said of man at first, that it was not good that he should be alone, so it is true of every believer. He is not to serve God alone, to think that a private religion is enough. Therefore, you have the examples of the first Christians, how they met with "one accord in one place"—to enjoy the public ordinances, pray together, have the Word preached to them, and receive the sacraments together (Acts 2:1; 5:12). And the apostle in 1 Corinthians 10:16–17 shows how the sacrament of the Lord's Supper declared their union and communion with one another. Thus, the apostle reproves those whose manner was not to assemble themselves together (Heb. 10:25).

This visible union of believers in church ordinances is their highest beauty and their greatest advantage. Hence David professes his ravishment in such unity, "How amiable are thy tabernacles, O LORD of hosts!" (Ps. 84:1). In Psalm 110, it is called "the beauties of holiness." And in Haggai 2, this temple is said to be more glorious than ever the former was, and that because of Christ's presence in it, preaching and reforming all abuses and corruptions. When the ark was taken, Eli's daughter-in-law cried, "The glory is departed from Israel" (1 Sam. 4:21). Hence the ordinances even in this life are called the kingdom of heaven because of God's glorious presence in them. David, when banished, longed to see the glory of God as he had seen it in the sanctuary (Ps. 63:2). And then it is our greatest profit and advantage, for God's presence is promised in them, so that the Christian ordinances are the life of the church. There is a larger dispensation of God's gifts and graces here than elsewhere.

Unity in the Government Christ Has Appointed in His Church

As God has appointed some to be shepherds and to govern, so He has appointed others to hear and obey. He has commanded admonition and, in some cases, sharp reproof, and where obstinacy is, He has commanded us to cast the member out. Now it is very hard to have unity in this respect, for as in 1 Corinthians 12, it appears that private Christians only keep within their sphere with difficulty. Every member desires to be an "eye," as the apostle there charges. So it is hard to be corrected by an obedient "ear," even if it gives a wise and godly reproof. It is therefore a blessed thing to have unity of order as well as of faith. That is, to see every member of the church in relation to one another in a harmonious way. This is how it is in the body. Though they are heterogeneous parts, yet they all associate harmoniously together in their operations. Such unity of order is like the nerves and ligaments of this spiritual society.

Unity in the Sympathy All Believers Have with One Another

This is so in respect of mourning and rejoicing. In respect of those that mourn, we are to weep and mourn with them. We are to bear one another's burdens. We are to be affected with the church's calamities because we are members of the same body. As the apostle said, "the care of all the churches" lay upon him. Who was afflicted, and he did not burn (2 Cor. 11:28–29)? The same sort of affection is to be in every believer proportionally. Therefore, this unity of believers should be vigorous in this way: whatever evil things happen to others, believers should be affected with them as if they are their own. This is evidence that they are lively members of the body. For if Christ, though in heaven, was conscious of the persecutions done by Paul against the church, saying, "Why persecutest thou me?" how much more should every particular member account the temptations of others as his own?

As it is thus for mourning, so also for rejoicing: there ought to be such unity among believers that we are to rejoice in the gifts, graces, and good things that others have, as if they were our own. But O the self-love, the envy, the complaining that are apt to be in one godly man against another. "The spirit that dwelleth in us lusteth to envy" (James 4:5), says the apostle, even in believers. This is why there are daily exhortations against begrudging, murmuring against, and envying one another. These are called the fruit of the flesh because where the Spirit of God works and enlivens there is joy, peace, and long-suffering, which are all graces contrary to such unquiet distempers. Now this is very difficult to flesh and blood: those parts and gifts which obscure yours, and those good things in others that seem to hinder yours, you ought to rejoice and bless God for them. You ought to do so as if it affected your own self. This spiritual and mystical unity will enable you to do so. Neither is the sun or air more requisite than this union; no wonder our Savior prays so movingly for it.

Unity in Mutually Striving Together to Promote the Kingdom and Glory of Christ

They all have the same heart, the same shoulders, and the same tongue to bless and praise God. They are like so many servants in the same house, all promoting and furthering their master's work. As the apostle says, all the officers are one—"He that planteth and he that watereth are one" (1 Cor. 3:8)—because they agree in one end: to set forward the work of God. Thus it is here, though there is so much variety in the gifts and graces, and conditions of God's people, yet they are all one in this work:

the glory of God is the end they all look upon. Thus you see into how many particulars this unity diffuses itself.

Invisible Unity Extends Further Than Visible Unity

The earlier mentioned sorts of unity are for the visible church only, but the latter are for the invisible. So that in this respect there is a unity between all believers that ever have been: with Enoch, Abel, Abraham, and all who ever were of old. This is confessed in what is usually called the Apostle's Creed: "I believe in the catholic [universal] church." Sometimes there was added, "the *one* catholic church," and this is something believed and not seen; but by this it stands that all the godly who have been, who are, and who ever shall be make up one body. All Christ's sheep will have one sheepfold. Therefore there is an invisible union where there cannot be a visible one.

Visible Unity Alone Is Not Enough

Now only those who are of this unity both visibly and invisibly truly enjoy God, are indeed members of Christ, and receive benefit by Him. But the other type are only Christian in name and title, like a withered branch in a tree, or an artificial eye or leg, which though joined to the body yet receives no life or nourishment from it. Do not think it is therefore enough to be of this visible unity; many have gloried and rested on this, that they are of such and such a church, yet their condemnation is greater than those of Sodom and Gomorrah.

Unity Must Begin with Christ

It is added, "that they also may be one in us" (John 17:21). This is because there must first be unity with Christ the Head, and then it extends to other members. This is to be considered the foundation and cause of it all. There must first be incorporation into Christ—"he that is joined unto the Lord is one spirit" with Him (1 Cor. 6:17).

Visible Unity Is Not Limited by Distance of Time and Place

Everyone is remembered in respect of prayer when the church is prayed for. So that the poor Christian who cannot pray for himself still has the prayers of the whole church of God. What a refreshing comfort this should be to every godly soul!

Application

Lay to heart more the divisions, differences, and breaches that are among the godly. Learn by Christ's example here to be affected with the unity of the church; again and again He commended peace to them. We are commanded to pray for the peace of Jerusalem. God is the God of peace, the gospel is the gospel of peace, and believers are called the children of peace. Take heed of being a Jonah in this ship; let not your pride, your conceits, or your discontent make you tear and rend the church. Pray that Jerusalem may be as a city compact together (Ps. 122:3).

CHAPTER 4

The Necessity of Christian Unity

"That they all may be one; as thou, Father, art in me, and I in thee" (John 17:21). We have declared the nature of this unity; let us now consider the excellence, benefit, and necessity of union among the godly.

It Is Christ's Passionate Prayer

The excellence and necessity of unity among Christians is made apparent by this vehement and affectionate prayer for it by the Savior. When He puts the whole company of believers together, He pitches upon this as the most eminent matter, that they may be one. And although our Savior had not the Spirit in measure, and so could not vainly repeat the same thing often, yet within a little space, He does four times mention this in John 17:21–23. Now certainly, the thing which our Savior (in whom are the treasures of all wisdom) greatly urged, must be of very great moment. It is not pardon of their sins, justification, adoption, glorification that is mentioned here, but unity. It is as if the whole kingdom of grace and glory consisted in this; obtain this and you have all. As our Savior prayed then, so He preached love and unity.

In relation to justification, He commended faith above all; in relation to sanctification, He includes everything under love. "A new commandment I give unto you, that ye love one another" (John 13:34). A new commandment—not that the duty was old, only envy and malice had so prevailed among the Jews—to love was a new thing, as if it had not been a duty required before. In John's epistles it is called both new and old (1 John 2:7–8). And then again new, because there are new motives, and a new pattern: "Love one another; as I have loved you" (John 13:34). There was never such a pattern and precedent before; so that it is not every kind of love and unity which answers Christ's prayer, but that which is in the highest degree of unity. It is added, "By this shall all men know ye are my disciples, if ye have love one to another" (John 13:35). Not if you work miracles or if you cast out devils but if you cast out discord and variance.

Therefore, there is not a greater scandal to religion and holiness than when those who believe are like the Levite's concubine, who was cut into many pieces. Again, "This is my commandment, that ye love one another, as I have loved you" (John 15:12). This is Christ's commandment, as if there were nothing else He required but this.

And as if this were not enough, in verse 17 He says, "These things I command you, that ye love one another," as if He should have said, "If bare information will not do it, if instruction will not do it, I lay My command and charge upon you."

It Is One Way to Bring the World to Believe the Truth

Secondly, this unity and love is a special means to bring the world to believe the truth and receive Christ. So that what the preaching of the Word and gifts—yes, miracles—used to do, unity and agreement may do. This is twice affirmed to be the consequence of unity, "That the world may believe that thou hast sent me" (John 17:21, 23). This is a special way to convince all the enemies of the truth: "By this shall all men know that ye are my disciples, if ye have love one to another" (John 13:35).

And do we not see by experience that heretics and all the profane are emboldened in their wickedness by nothing more than the differences and opinions of those who are godly? Do they not in books and otherwise in derision say that one sect has the Spirit of God, while another says they have the Spirit, and yet both are contrary to one another? Can the Spirit of God be contrary to Himself? Can He be a Spirit of truth in one and a spirit of falsehood in others? Now although this is not a good argument, because the Spirit of God is communicated only in measure to the godly (therefore they know only in part, and so they love only in part, and there are many errors and divisions we are prone to), yet this is a very great stumbling block. Therefore woe to that godly man who by his pride, self-conceit, or erroneous doctrine brings such a scandal to religion! What if many perish in hell because of your stubborn spirit?

It is true, there ought to be zeal against errors and corruptions, even in the godly. You see that when Peter did not walk right, Paul resisted him to the face, and would not give place to him, or other false teachers—no, not for an hour (Gal. 2:5). Mark that, no, not for an hour. Some think, "Let them alone, they will recover themselves, they will do no hurt, truth needs not be afraid." Yet Paul was afraid that an hour's forbearance might do hurt. Therefore he adds, "that the truth of the gospel might continue with you," as if an hour's forbearance might hinder the continuance of truth. So we are to use scriptural zeal and scriptural means to convince even those that are godly, when they err in doctrine.

Therefore, the Scripture does not commend the kind of unity and love which lets all errors and profaneness alone, but unity in that which is good, unity in that which is truth and holiness. It is that which Christ means here in His prayer, and where this unity is, which is very potent to win all who contradict it. It is admirable to mollify the hearts of the opposers. This is why it is so often reported of the early Christians that they were daily with one accord together. The evangelist

Luke records this at least five times. So if nothing else will make you tender about causing any breaches in the church of God, this should: that by causing divisions you are doing as much as lies in you to hinder anyone who knows you ever to believe and to be converted.

It Is Promised

Thirdly, this unity is promised as a special part of the covenant of grace. The very covenant which promises to write the law of God in our hearts, and to put His fear in our inward parts, also promises unity at the same time. "They shall be my people, and I will be their God: and I will give them one heart, and one way, that they may fear me for ever" (Jer. 32:38–39). This is one main term in the covenant of grace. "In that day shall there be one LORD, and his name one" (Zech. 14:9). The meaning is that they shall not worship many gods, or serve in different ways of worship, but they shall be one. To this purpose Ezekiel also prophesies (Ezek. 37:16, 22), a prophecy which is not to be limited to the Jews only but also to all the believing Gentiles.

Oh then in these times of differences and breaches among the godly, where should we turn? What should we plead in prayer but these promises? "O Lord, to be divided, to have altar against altar, church against church, prophet against prophet—is this what it means to have one heart, and one way? Make good Thy promise!"

It Is Spiritually Helpful

Fourthly, unity is necessary, because hereby a service-able and beneficial mutual assistance in spiritual things is preserved. The people of God are compared to living stones built up together: while the stones remain in the building, they support one another, but if they are removed, it falls down. They are compared to members in the body: while they are joined together, there is a mutual ministration to each other, but when divided from the body, no part can receive any nourishment. So it is here. While the people of God are in union, oh the wonderful help they are to one another! They provoke one another to good works and they stir up one another's graces. But take these coals away from one another and then the fire goes out!

And this may be the reason why our Savior does not mention the sanctification and holiness of believers but rather mentions their unity, because unity is a special means of preserving and increasing holiness. "Two are better than one," because of heat and of help, says the wise man (Eccl. 4:9–12); and so it is in this work of grace: two are better than one to warm one another. How greatly your zeal might help against another's luke-warmness, and your faith against another's diffidence! If it is so great a sin to see your brother in temporal need and not relieve him, how much more is it a sin to see him in spiritual need and fail to help him? "If a man be overtaken in a fault, ye which are spiritual, restore such an one" (Gal. 6:1). Put this bone in joint again.

Experience tells us that where there are divisions and discord, there is no love, no compassion, no watching over one another. If this unity were established, a man would then strive for the growth of grace in others, as in himself. And therefore observe that the power of godliness greatly abates when differences arise. There is not that heavenly communion, nor hearty concurrence in the ways of holiness, nor that mutual help of one another, as at other times.

It Sanctifies

Unity among the godly is so necessary that God many times permits sad and heavy persecutions to befall them, so that in this way their discords and divisions may be removed and they may be more endeared to one another. Times of prosperity in the church made the greatest heresies and schisms, but the times of bloody persecution made the godly more united. Thus the martyrs, some of them in Queen Mary's days, bewailed their differences and the contests they formerly had with one another, but prison and persecution made them highly prize one another. Joseph's brethren in their plenty envied and fell out with one another, but in their distress they were glad to cleave together. If sheep are scattered from one another, when a sudden storm arises it makes them all huddle together. It may be that although just now the godly are so censorious, so shy, so strange to one another, God may in time work so that they will be glad to enjoy one another, glad to have communion with each other. One godly man's company may then be worth more to you than the gold of Ophir. If love and godliness do not unite you, take heed lest God sends some outward trouble and affliction to put you together. If you do not embrace one another willingly, He may bind you in His chains together. His promise to Judah and Israel, of making the two sticks one, was after the cruel enmity and opposition which had been among them (Ezek. 37).

It Strengthens

Unity confirms and establishes the church. The old rule is that strength united is stronger. Sunbeams united together send out greater heat. It is union in an army, in a nation, in any society, that preserves it. As a wise man said, public societies are immortal if they do not kill themselves by division. Our Savior confirmed this when He said, "Every city or house divided against itself shall not stand" (Matt. 12:25). He brings this in as an argument to show that He did not cast out devils by the help of devils but by the Spirit of God. Thus, if the people of God cast out error and profaneness by God's Spirit, then they will not entertain error and profaneness themselves; for this would be to set a kingdom at variance within itself. The old rule is "Divide and conquer."

It was a unique providence that Christ's bones should not be broken, to demonstrate by this (some say) that though Christ died yet He did not lose His strength. We must justly fear that God has some heavy scourge on the godly when they are first divided. If their bones are broken, their strength is weakened, but their evil and misery will not stop there.

Thus, it is a very foolish and weak thing in the godly to continue in their divisions, for do they not have mighty and numberless enemies? Does not the whole world hate them? Is not the world like wolves to the godly, who are like sheep? Now if not only the wolf and the fox but also one sheep shall devour another, must not this bring utter ruin? The apostle Paul speaks fully to this, "If ye bite and devour one another, take heed that ye be not consumed one of another" (Gal. 5:15). Observe the notable expression, "bite and devour one another." How unnatural this is to sheep! It is dogs that do this! And further, by this means you will consume one another. What the devils of hell and all your wicked adversaries could not do, you will do to one another. Do not look on your differences as mere sins, but as heavy omens of God's wrath. When the veil in the temple was rent in pieces, this was a presage of the destruction of the temple.

It Is Beautiful

Seventhly, unity is a most comely and beautiful thing to see. It is a ravishing thing to behold such a harmony among the godly! Therefore, the completeness of it will be in heaven. There those many thousands will all have one heart and one tongue to praise God. There will be no difference. One shall not have one way of seeing God, and another, another way. There will be no censuring, such as using reproachful terms against one another. Now the nearer the people of God come to this on earth, the more similar they are to glorified saints in heaven, and to those innumerable companies of angels that do God's will. The angels have no jarring and contests; one angel is not of one opinion, and another of another. We ought to do God's will as the angels do it, not only in respect of zeal and purity, but in respect of unity also.

One of the Songs of Ascents is entirely in praise of unity (Psalm 133). Unity is compared to the precious ointment that was to be composed so carefully that no one was permitted to presume to make similar oil. It was only to be poured on the high priest. The psalmist also compares unity to the fruitful and pleasant dew on the mountains. The whole psalm is remarkable:

(a) Unity is for us to "behold." The psalm begins with "behold" to draw others to admire it (Ps. 133:1). As if to say, "You have seen by bitter experience what disputes and differences produce, now look at this!"

(b) It is "good" and "pleasant." Profit and pleasure win everyone. By this we can see our aversion to such unity that we need those low arguments to draw us. The psalmist does not say it is just, holy, and acceptable to God, but simply that it is good and pleasant.

(c) It is "for brethren." He does not say "men" but rather "brethren," because sinful discord is apt to creep in amongst them.

(d) It is "together." He does not speak of togetherness of location but togetherness of soul. The sweetness of this unity is represented by the oil that was poured on Aaron and then ran down. It must be a peace grounded on Christ, our Head and High Priest, which then should diffuse itself to others. Its profitableness is described by the dew. It is from heaven and so sanctifies the barren ground. This concord is God's gift only, and if received, it wonderfully blesses the church.

Who would not have rejoiced to live in the days when all believers were of one heart and one soul? What a comfort it would have been to hear no grudging or repining at one another! But the devil (that envious one) quickly sowed tares among them. Ulcers and sores appeared on that body which once was as beautiful as Absalom's body. So the apostles press greatly that all things should be done in charity, that they fulfill the royal law by loving, and that they do not even grudge one another. This unity and peace is so glorious that the apostle makes it a goal: "Study [or be ambitious] to be quiet" (1 Thess. 4:11). There is a great deal of carnal and worldly ambition after things that are fading and transitory. Here is godly and spiritual ambition: to be a peacemaker. To be a peace-preserver is the greatest glory God puts on us.

It Is in the Nature of the Godly

This duty of love and uniting is naturally built into the hearts of the godly. It should be that which they are most persuaded of and most inclined to. It is strange if you were to say, "God has taught me such and such high things and has not taught me love." The apostle speaks excellently: "As touching brotherly love ye need not that I write unto you: for ye yourselves are taught of God to love one another" (1 Thess. 4:9). It is a shame and a reproach to us that we need a sermon for this. Oh fear yourself! You boast of the teachings of God's Spirit above what others have, and yet you are not taught to love!

Some people think that the preaching ministry is needless and they will not hear it. If nothing else convinces them of the need of it, yet this may, that God has not taught them the duty of love enough, and therefore they need the ministers of God to do it. But by this you see that love and unity should be so planted in all the godly that we would not need to press and preach this any more than a hungry man needs to be urged to eat his food, or the mother to love her child. God teaches this duty in the chief place.

It Is in the Nature of Religion

All other things in religion are reduced to one and agree in unity. Everything in religion tends to this. Why should the people of God not embrace it? The various unities in religion are used by the apostle to make a notable argument in Ephesians 4. Having exhorted believers to walk worthy of their calling in verse 1, the apostle gives instances of the graces that procure unity: "with all lowliness and meekness...forbearing one another" (Eph. 4:2). These graces are the comely, worthy graces of our holy calling. You have the purpose of these graces in verse 3, "endeavouring [making it our aim, labor, study, and prayer] to keep the unity of the Spirit in the bond of peace."

Then he enumerates in Ephesians 4:4 why there should be such unity: "There is one body." Christ does not have many bodies, any more than anybody else has. The whole people of God are one body. How destructive it is when one part of the body should conspire against the welfare of another! Let grace do in this spiritual body what nature does in the physical body.

Then, there is "one Spirit." There is but one Spirit that enlightens and sanctifies the whole church of God. Why then should there be so many contrary opinions and ways which pretend to be from the same Spirit? Indeed, the apostle says, there are a diversity of gifts and operations yet there is the same Spirit. He does not say there are contrarieties and the same Spirit—that is as impossible as for darkness to come from the sun! If then there is only one Spirit, the godly must not give an opportunity to the Enemy to blaspheme, as they already do by saying that the Calvinistic spirit is one thing and . the Lutheran spirit another.

Again, there is "one hope of your calling"; we are called to one inheritance. There is only one heaven prepared for all the godly. Why then should they be so different on the way, when at our journey's end we must all be received into the same place of glory? It is true, our Savior says that in His Father's house are many mansion places (John 14:2). But although there is room enough for all, yet there is only one house. If one church cannot contain us now, how do we think one heaven will?

It follows in Ephesians 4:5 that there is "one Lord," that is, Christ, who is to be worshiped and served by us. Indeed if there were many lords, as the Roman Catholics make many saints in heaven for worship, it would be no wonder if this led to several faiths and forms of worship. But the Lord Christ is one. The apostle urged the Corinthians to reconcile their divisions in this way: "Is Christ divided?" (1 Cor. 1:13). Unless there are many Christs, or Christ is divided into many parts, there ought not to be many divisions in the church. How absurd it would be to say, I have one Christ, while someone else says that he has another, and a third person says he has a third Christ?

There is one faith, one system of doctrine to be believed. All the different details make up one entire truth. Although there are many religions and faiths in the world, yet indeed there is only one. The apostle says there are many that are called gods—gods in name—"but to us there is but one God" (1 Cor. 8:5–6). There are many that are called religions, many called churches, but indeed there is only one.

The next argument is that there is "one baptism," one profession of the doctrine of faith. There is one kind of baptism, though there are many administrations of baptism. Christ has appointed only one way for the profession of His name, and one way for His being called on by us. The sacrament of the Lord's Supper is also an argument for unity (1 Cor. 10:17). The sacraments have unity in their meaning; they manifest one body and one Spirit. How sad it is that there should be so many divisions in the church about sacraments, which are the seals of unity and communion!

Lastly, there is "one God and Father of all" (Eph. 4:6). Because there is only one God, we ought therefore to seek unity. God is one and cannot be divided in Himself. He cannot command things to be believed or done contrary to Himself.

Let all these unities therefore make us serious in striving for unity. There is unity in hell, where all the devils agree against the church. It was possible to have a legion of devils in one man; shall there then be unity against us, and we not have unity among ourselves?

CHAPTER 5

The Reasons for the Lack of Christian Unity

Divisions Are the Fruit of the Flesh

Divisions and differences are the fruit of the flesh. Love, peace, and kindness are the fruit of the Spirit. Thus, a man cannot demonstrate himself to be in the flesh and devoid of God's Spirit by anything other than a contentious, divisive spirit. Some people are restless; they cannot live without an enemy. But such people only demonstrate their nature and show who their father is—the devil, the envious one, who delights to sow tares among the wheat.

The two main principles of people's actions in the world are described in Galatians 5:19–23, the flesh and the Spirit. The one is completely opposed to the other. Observe what the works of the one and the other are. The works of the flesh are hatred, variance, strife, emulations, etc., all tending to break unity. The works of the Spirit are entirely contrary: love, peace, gentleness, etc., all uniting graces. If you want to know who a godly

man is and who has the Spirit of God, judge the tree by
its fruit. The godly man is full of love, gentleness, and
meekness. It is impossible that pride, arrogance, and
envying should be the fruit of God's Spirit. Thus, the
apostle argues, if "there is among you envying, and strife,
and divisions, are ye not carnal?" (1 Cor. 3:3).

Thus the apostle James speaks notably about this.
"Who is a wise man and endued with knowledge among
you? let him shew out of a good conversation his works
with meekness of wisdom" (James 3:13). James divides
wisdom into that which is (a) earthly and devilish, the
mother of envying and strife, and (b) the wisdom from
above, which is first pure and then peaceable. Those who
have a name for religion are nevertheless still troubled by
this evil spirit (James 3:15–16). The apostle urges them to
"glory not, and lie not against the truth" (v. 14). Though a
man pretends to have the most unique gifts and extraordinary teachings of God's Spirit, yet if he is contentious,
he is not to glory, and in fact, he lies against the truth.
You might say that it is for the truth you are contentious;
that it is for the truth you have made these divisions. No,
the truths of Christ are to be maintained by the Spirit
of Christ. As the wrath of man does not work the righteousness of God, so neither does the perverseness of
man work the truths of God. As far then as any in the
church of God are contentious and striving, thus far they
demonstrate the power of the flesh reigning in them.

Why Are There So Many Divisions among the Godly?

We must cry out in language that is directly opposite to the psalmist; we say, "Behold how sad and destructive a thing it is for brethren to be at discord with one another!" How is it that the godly forget the spirit they are of? They do not consider that the Spirit of God descended in the shape of a dove. Babel was to be built by a confusion of languages but Jerusalem was to be built without any noise of the hammer. Solomon had to build the temple, not David, because David had been a man of war.

Let us answer the following objection. Since God has promised one heart and one way, and since Christ has also prayed so earnestly for it (and He is not refused anything by the Father), how is it there are so many breaches among the godly?

Sin Creates Division

Though unity among the godly is necessary, yet even the promise and the prayer imply that there will necessarily be divisions and oppositions to the world. We are not to wonder if the gospel and the powerful dispensing of Christ's ways makes factions and troubles in the world, for the godly cannot have peace with themselves without being in open opposition to the world. In this chapter and in other places our Savior informs them that the world will hate them. So we are not to say that the gospel of Christ is in itself of a turbulent dividing nature, as carnal politicians suggest, and that therefore the best peace and unity is where atheism abounds. For if by the gospel there are sad distractions and concussions of kingdoms and states, it is not from the genius of the gospel but from the opposition and corruption of men's hearts.

Therefore, when our Savior said He came to send fire and sword in the earth, that father should be against son, and mother against daughter, and that a man's enemies should be those of his own house (Luke 12:52–53), this was not from the nature of Christ's doctrine but from the corrupt infirmity of the sinner. When the sun hurts sore eyes, or when medicine taken disturbs the body fluids and makes a man sicker, in these cases it is not the sun or the physician who is to be blamed. So if the introduction of Christ's kingdom and His ordinances make great divisions in a place, it is not Christ's way but wicked men's sins that are to be blamed. This then is to be concluded, that the godly and the wicked can have no unity. The godly will not come round to the world's principles, and the world will not come round to the godly one's principles, and therefore there must be a perpetual enmity. This made the wise man say that the righteous was an abomination to the wicked, and the wicked to the righteous (Prov. 29:27).

Wicked Men Create Division

Though there cannot be unity between sheep and wolves, the godly and the wicked, yet even in the church of God there are many who still retain their beastly nature, and though they have the title of Christians, yet they are really of the devil. Hence, in Christ's church there is often such deadly opposition. Little wonder then if among those who claim to highly reverence Christ there are nevertheless sad divisions, for many are still in the flesh; many do not experimentally savor the things of God. "Of your own selves shall men arise, speaking perverse things," says the apostle (Acts 20:30). Similarly, "there shall be false teachers among you, who privily shall bring in damnable heresies" (2 Peter 2). And why? Because they are "men of corrupt minds" (2 Tim. 3:8).

If then all who claim to be Christ's people, and to have His Spirit, did in reality have Christ's Spirit, there would be no such divisions. But as the apostle says, "They went out from us, but they were not of us" (1 John 2:19), and, "there must be also heresies among you, that they which are approved may be made manifest among you" (1 Cor. 11:19).

Therefore, though Christ has prayed for unity, and God has promised unity, yet the church will still be grievously torn, because some who are *in* the church are not *of* the church, and therefore they are not included in God's promise or Christ's prayer. Hence it is that the Scripture is full of predictions like this—that there shall arise false prophets, that there shall be wolves in sheep's clothes, that Satan will transform himself into an angel of light, by which, if it were possible, the very elect will be seduced.

Therefore, you are not to reason when you see raging divisions among those that profess faith in Christ and holiness, that Christ has prayed in vain, or that there is no truth, no religion at all. Rather you are to realize that there are many hypocrites in the church—many who, for their pride and rebellion against the light, and for other sins, are left by God, and given up to believe a lie. From such differences, let us conclude with this pious meditation, that even under the known light of the gospel people may sadly apostatize, and become heretics—and even persecutors of the truth—if the Spirit of God does not keep them in a holy fear. Therefore, in the midst of these differences realize that there is an apparent believer, an apparent church, an apparent professor. And it is common for such, for some corrupt end or other, to make a breach in Christ's body.

Unity Exists in Relation to Salvation

There is unity in fundamental matters relating to salvation. Now when God has promised and Christ has prayed for the sanctification of His people, by this they are seen to have as much grace as shall certainly bring them to heaven. For though they do not have all the degrees of grace, and neither are freed from all sin, yet they have the essence of grace, that will certainly bring them to eternal glory. So it is in unity. Although in many things they have not attained to the same mind, to the same judgment, yet they all agree in the things that are necessary to salvation, and this is called "all truth." "The Spirit of truth…will guide you into all truth" (John 16:13), and they have the unction which teaches them all things (1 John 2:20). Hence, it is not possible to deceive the elect—that is, in fundamental things—things that exclude salvation when they are denied. It is true, the disciples doubted a while about Christ's resurrection, which was a fundamental point, but it is one thing to doubt something, and another thing heretically to oppose it. The godly cannot live and die in a fundamental error no more than in a gross sin unrepented of, because fundamental errors necessarily oppose salvation. This may be a great comfort to the godly under the diversity of opinions and the several subtle ways of those who would bring in damnable heresies.

Unity Will Be Consummated in Heaven

Even in lesser principles their unity shall be consummated in heaven. We must understand Christ's prayer here, as in His other petitions, as reaching to heaven, where all grace and holiness will be completed. The comfort is that one day all the godly will lay aside their bitterness and their censures of one another, and they will all with one mouth, and in one way, praise and glorify God without any difference at all.

Ignorance Creates Division

Christ has not given His Spirit to the church in its full measure in this life, and therefore believers know but in part, they love but in part. Now all division arises from ignorance in the mind and corruption in the heart. As long therefore as these relics of ignorance and corruption shall be in us, so long will these divisions last. As long as the earth emits vapors, so long will thunder and lightning be in the air.

The Devil Creates Division

Lastly, the devil is still wielding his power, and his work is to fill the church with differences, and to raise up instruments to cause differences, so that his kingdom may the more prosper. Therefore, though heretical incendiaries are taken away, yet because the devil does not die, therefore he is still setting his cloven foot where God has raised up any church.

CHAPTER 6

The Characteristics of Christian Unity

*That they all may be one; as thou, Father, art in me,
and I in thee.*
—John 17:21

Next regarding Christian unity are some cautions of which we must beware. The name of unity, like the name of peace, is very deceptive and misleadingly attractive. Jerome said, "Cursed be that peace which forsakes the truth." Likewise, cursed be that unity which damages the kingdom of Christ. It is possible to paint over sinful confederacy in ways of sin as though this was the glorious unity commended by Christ.

A Unity from and to Christ

The unity which Christ commends and prays for comes from Christ originally. It culminates in Him and the things that are His: His truth, His ways, and

His commands. Any unity that does not begin there, and result in those things, is a sinful and wicked unity. There is an antichristian unity. The Roman Catholics glory in their unity, the fact that they all acknowledge one way, and indeed they make it a mark of their church. All wicked men in the world are united as one man in opposing what is godly.

Now such unity is a matter of shame and mourning. For one thing, it is not terminated on Christ. They have not first been united to the true head. This oil is not first on Aaron's head (Psalm 133). Instead they are of the devil, who moves and reigns in their hearts. And for another thing, it is not a unity in the way Scripture describes. It is not a union in the true doctrine, but in heresy—not a union in the instituted worship of God, but in idolatry and superstition. It is a union aspiring to overthrow Christ's kingdom, if this were possible. We must therefore examine the cause and aim of our unity; otherwise it will afford no true comfort.

A Directed and Ordered Unity

Christian unity must be a directed and ordered unity. This unity must not be confusion. The chaos and unformed heap which God created at first was one thing, but it was confused, it was without form. A house demolished makes one heap, but it is a ruinous, disordered heap. Similarly, scriptural unity is one which keeps the order and distinction God has appointed.

Indeed, we should greatly emphasize this point in case, under the pretense that all the people of God are one, we should introduce confusion, and make Christ's body a horrendously deformed monster. Though the church is the one body of Christ, yet in it there are distinct members, and all have their different roles. The apostle argues against those who would confuse this order. Are all the members of the body an eye? (1 Cor. 12:14–16). This kind of confusion has often sorely troubled the church. Through pride and for corrupt reasons people have not kept the order and distinction which God has made in His church. This is why the apostle so often presses the people to hear, to obey, to submit themselves to their leaders, and to have them in high esteem for their work's sake (1 Thess. 5:13). And the reason for all this is that, while this unity of order is preserved, the church itself and godliness is preserved.

A Gracious Unity

Christian unity is consistent even with the graces that have an outward appearance of dissolving unity, such as zeal for the glory of God, sharp and severe reproof of those who go astray, and no toleration of heresies or profaneness in those who are of the church after they have been admonished. There is a sinful and foolish pity when people do not wish to have justice done against notorious offenders, but this pity to the wicked is in reality cruelty to the good—for anyone who is pitiful to the wolf is cruel to the sheep.

So there is a counterfeit unity and love when, because of this false peace and agreement, no damnable heresy and no evil way is treated with the severity it deserves, and no scriptural way is taken to stop its progress. If this were true Christian unity, then Ahab would have been right to call Elijah a troubler of Israel when Elijah's zeal would not bear the idolatries then practiced. If this was true Christian unity, then all the godly prophets would justly have been discouraged by their opposition when they reproved the sinful ways of the times they lived in. For that matter, Christ Himself and His apostles would justly be condemned, because the zeal of God ate them up to such an extent that they reproved not only the gross idolatries, but also almost every petty form of superstition.

The apostle Paul so often commended the spirit of love and meekness, desiring that there would be no hatred or strife among them. Then when he says, "I would they were even cut off which trouble you" (Gal. 5:12), and, "whose mouths must be stopped…teaching things which they ought not" (Titus 1:11), are we to imagine that he has forgotten his own rule and become an incendiary in the church? The apostle John insists on love in every verse, and shows that he who hates his brother is like Cain, a murderer, and of the devil. Then when he says, "If there come any unto you, and bring not this doctrine, receive him not into your house, neither bid him God speed" (2 John 10), are we to imagine that now he has forgotten his own spirit, and that his sweetness is turned into bitterness?

We should then be fully persuaded that the unity and love which Christ prays for is not inconsistent with scriptural zeal and courage against profane and erroneous ways. It does not bring in a compliance with profaneness and co-confessing with heresies. It does not build a temple, as the Romans did, to all gods, nor make the church like the ark, into which both clean and unclean animals were received. No, such remissness breaks unity, just as the strings of a harp cannot make any melodious sound when they are not well wound up, and paralyzed limbs, for lack of the due strength, cause many feeble operations.

CHAPTER 7

The Rules for Christian Unity

Having established the characteristics of Christian unity, let us consider what remedies are fit to heal inevitable wounds. As in the natural body, a wound damages that which should be whole, so it is in the spiritual body of the church. Unless there is wisdom and skill, wounds are made worse by doctors. Likewise, unless proportionate and appropriate remedies are applied with wisdom and compassion, the breach in Christian unity is made greater.

False Remedies

First, there are two false remedies which we need to beware of. They are at opposite extremes. One is a rigid and inflexible uniformity, and the other is an unbridled acceptance of all sorts of ideas and practices.

Absolute Uniformity

The first false remedy is a rigid, imperious, and tyranni-cal commanding of uniformity and approbation in every tiny detail, so that no dissent or liberty is allowed—even to someone humble and peaceable who earnestly desires to find out the truth. This is the remedy suggested by the Roman Catholic Church. This tyranny came into the church early on.

Certainly, in matters of less concern, where people may err *without* compromising the faith, or when people build only hay and stubble, not laying other foundations, the apostle commands charitable behavior between the strong Christian and the weak (Romans 14). It is true too that even the least truth of Christ is precious, and we are not to deny it. Yet it is not to be forced on people, even if eternal damnation is inevitable if that truth is not received. Our Savior says that if new wine is put into old bottles, the bottles break (Matt. 9:17). People impose opinions or practices of less consequence on a people not prepared; then, instead of unity, they make many factions.

Yet this false way of imposing unity has often infested the church, and especially when authorities have vested interests. They insist on unity not so much out of love to Christ as to further their own interest. As the soldiers who did not want to have Christ's coat divided, everyone was hoping to have it all. So when Luther reformed, the church authorities preached constantly about the church as the seamless coat of Christ. But this entire endeavor to have such uniformity was not out of love to Christ's church, but to keep their own power. The reason they were afraid of divisions was fear of having their kingdom overthrown. "Either subscribe or leave," used to be a common saying. Certainly those who impose unity in such an austere and severe way should be reminded of what Augustine said: "Let them rage and persecute who know not with what prayers and tears it is given to understand but a little of God's truth."

Unbounded Toleration

There is another false way of unity, extremely opposed to the method of rigid unity. That is, a licentious and unbounded toleration of damnable heresies and idolatries. The Roman emperor Julian, also known as Julian the Apostate, studiously promoted this method of unity in the fourth century, intending in this way to overthrow the Christian religion. It has also been strenuously championed by Socinians, who deny the divinity of Christ. Now, just as rigid uniformity tends to have been advocated by those who had power in the church, so those who have been the oppressed party advocate this licentious toleration. Neither extreme is scriptural.

The "angels" or ministers of the church are commended in Scripture when they did not tolerate, or could not bear, those who published unsound doctrine, and those who did tolerate heresy are reproved (Revelation 2–3). It is important to note that these are ministers of the church, for we are talking about church peace and liberty, not political and external peace and liberty, which is not included in Christ's petition for unity among His people. Certainly, the apostles in their epistles are set against false doctrines and false teachers, at least as much, if not more, as they speak out against corrupt practices. Hymenaeus and Alexander were delivered up to Satan for their blasphemies and false doctrines (1 Tim. 1:20). And the universal rule is given, "An heretick after the first and second admonition reject" (Titus 3:10). So it is very clear that church power and church censures are to be applied to those who obstinately offend by propagating false doctrine.

A boundless toleration of all kind of heresies is seen to be such a harsh and unattractive thing that even the Remonstrants, or Dutch Arminians, disavow it, even though they called for a liberty of prophesying. Even they professed that along with the liberty to hold all sorts of opinions there ought to be efforts made to root out heresies. This licentiousness then does not beget unity but increases breaches, for it gives scope for people's corruptions to vent them. It is like the warm summer to snakes and serpents, which makes them come out and spread their poison, when the cold winter kept them in.

True Remedies

Now that we have dismissed these false remedies, let us consider what are true and proper remedies. What oil is fit to be poured into the church's wounds, seeing it is so often like the man who was attacked by robbers on the way to Jericho? These remedies counter three attacks against unity: (1) healing division in doctrine caused by heresy, (2) healing division in godly order caused by schism, and (3) healing division in Christian love caused by contentiousness.

Unity in Doctrine

1. Nourish Essential Unity

So far as there is an agreement in judgment, we should close in with each other heartily, and embrace one another in that agreement. It is a mercy that differences between the godly are not in the very fundamentals and vitals of religion. Seeing therefore that there are common opinions and doctrines which the godly agree upon, let that unity be nourished. This is one means to produce further union.

This rule is given by the apostle, "If in any thing ye be otherwise minded, God shall reveal even this unto you. Nevertheless, whereto we have already attained, let us walk by the same rule" (Phil. 3:15–16). It is great obstinacy in the Lutherans that they will not acknowledge the Calvinists as brethren, even though they may agree with each other in the fundamental truths of the Christian faith.

To the extent then that people retain Christ and fundamental truth with a humble, godly disposition, desiring to be further informed, do not let the lack of what they should have make you despise the good things they have.

2. Esteem Godly Ministers

Individual Christians should highly esteem and submit to the godly and faithful pastors God has set over them. For commonly the breach begins when people begin to be offended at faithful pastors. It was some misunderstanding about what Christ preached that made so many disciples forsake Him. It was a "hard speech," they said, and they were not interested in coming to a better understanding.

When people will not acknowledge the public office which God has appointed, they wander into wrong paths. Here you see the twofold purpose of the ministers of Christ—the one is to keep people from being carried about with every wind of doctrine, and the other is for spiritual edification, "till we all come in the unity of the faith" (Eph. 4:12–13). Therefore a due and fit obedience and acknowledgment of the pastors God has given would, in a special manner, prevent divisions.

3. Pity Those Who Go Astray

Exhibit a pitiful and compassionate spirit to those who go astray. We are indeed to have zeal, and a holy impatience with what is wrong in the church of God, yet this is to be accompanied with pity. "And of some have compassion, making a difference," says the apostle Jude (v. 22).

Certainly, when we consider how prone we are to receive error for truth, how naturally blind and opposite our minds are to the revealed truths of God, how it is the Spirit of God that leads us into truth, and how God keeps us from the heresies and errors that others are carried aside with—these things will greatly move us to tenderheartedness toward others.

4. Avoid Misrepresenting What Others Believe

(a) If we report the opinions of those who dissent from us, we must do so candidly and truly. Nothing makes the gap wider, and twists the knife more into the wounds of the church than a malevolent disposition to pervert other people's opinions, to claim that they hold monstrous things, which in reality they detest with all their hearts.

It has been thought that this was the reason why the apostle James wrote that epistle arguing for works as well as faith, because some misunderstood Paul's writings—as if Paul had taught that faith only was enough to save, even though it was not accompanied with a holy life. How often were Christ and the apostles traduced for preaching things they never taught!

Malicious enemies, desiring to make them more offensive and to bring them into greater danger, did this. And are not Protestants to this very day represented as if they were the most damnable and blasphemous heretics that ever were? But if it is not lawful in civil matters to bear false witness against another, much less is it permissible in religious and doctrinal matters.

Whether therefore it is by writing, preaching, report, or any other way God's Word and conscience requires of us, we are to represent the opinions of others honestly and accurately. We must not put a sense of our own on their opinions, and then fight with that. This is not the way to bring the straying sheep back again. This will never bring us back to unity, for those who dissent from us will soon see that it is not truth we are seeking but victory—and that our purpose is not to bring them to the knowledge of truth, but to disgrace and defame them. This will never win them over.

Therefore it is necessary in all disputations to state the controversy accurately. If you get it wrong to start with, it never gets mended afterward. People may write voluminous books and bring multitudes of arguments, all to no purpose if the true state of the controversy is not laid down. To know the true and proper distance between you and those who dissent from you is the only way to have a hope of uniting eventually, just as the best way to recover from a disease is to be truly informed what it is.

(b) As well as accurately representing other people's views, we should also take care not to impose conclusions and inferences on their doctrines that do not properly and genuinely flow from them.

It is not fair to attribute something to them as their doctrine which is actually only our inference, an inference that we may have made through ignorance or any other failing. It is especially unfair if they abhor such conclusions with their whole soul. There were spiders that sucked poison from even those sweet herbs which the apostle had planted, because he showed that where sin had abounded grace abounded much more. They then forced this consequence on the apostle's doctrine— to sin "that grace may abound" (Rom. 6:1). Certainly, the evident and plain consequence of a doctrine is to be accounted of as the doctrine itself. As we know, whatever is a clear, genuine consequence from Scripture is Scripture, but this is not the case with every consequence we are apt to deduce. So it is with other people's opinions. What is evidently a consequence from any doctrine, we may attribute it to the doctrine, but we must be sure that it is the proper and natural child, not some illegitimate offspring, the true issue and not merely our own suppositions.

5. Be Careful How We Publicize Our Own Opinions

If there is a truth God has made known to us, or if we have reasoned something out for ourselves, we are to be very careful how we publicize it. This has been constant fire in the church of God when people have either received or reasoned out some doctrine different from the current way of the church at that time. It is a very hard thing to be (so to speak) pregnant, and not to be eager to have the child delivered to the world. People are called heretics because they insist on choosing their own way, obstinately raising damnable doctrines. Heretics invent and devise a doctrine of their own, and are therefore compared to thieves and robbers who do not go in by the door but climb up some other way.

If you think you have found a new truth, qualifications such as the following are necessary.

(a) Question and examine your own spirit, instead of immediately believing your own heart. It is a firebrand in the church when people have no modest doubts and questions of their own ignorance and proneness to err even in things they are so confident of. How modestly the apostle Paul speaks when he determined the question about marriage, "I think also that I have the Spirit of God" (1 Cor. 7:40). He distinguishes between what he had as an express command from the Lord, and what he was inwardly directed to. Wherever the Spirit of God leads into all truth, there He likewise leads into all humility.

(b) Before you publish it to the world, communicate your thoughts to those who are able, wise, and learned in the church of God. They have the Spirit of God and

His unction as well as we. Paul, though he was called directly by Christ, yet went up to Jerusalem to confer with the chief pillars of the church there. And though he was miraculously converted, yet he needed to go to Ananias to be further directed. Those who had extraordinary gifts were nevertheless to submit themselves to others.

Paul also tells us, "The spirits of the prophets are subject to the prophets" (1 Cor. 14:32). This is interpreted in two ways, both of which are relevant to us. It may mean that the spirit of the prophets is subject to other prophets, that is, other prophets have power to judge the doctrine they publish. If so, then it follows with much greater force that what we (who are not prophets) have in an ordinary way should be exposed to the examination of others. Alternatively, we may understand this saying to mean that no prophet who has the Spirit of God moving in him is so extraordinarily wrought upon but he may restrain those motions of the Spirit, and vent them in an orderly way—for example, by not speaking while others are speaking. This seems to be the general thrust of what the apostle is saying in that place. This is very relevant to my point, that no one can have revelations and impulses from God's Spirit without having a divine method and good order to declare them. For publishing some things in the wrong time and way is like good medicine which is not administered in its fit season.

6. Value the Clear and Familiar Truths about Christ
Lastly, a special means of keeping up the unity of faith is to highly prize and delight in the known plain truths of Christ. Paul was taken up to the third heavens, yet he desired to know nothing but Christ crucified. Peter thought it was not inconvenient to write the same things they knew already. Certainly nothing has more rent and torn the church of God than people claiming to have unique revelations about high things—to bring in some unheard of and unknown truths! Oh, how proud it would make some people to have it said that *they* were the first to have said it! But to be weary of the known truth is in effect to be weary of the same God, the same Christ. We might as well desire a new sun, a new earth, and a new world as well!

Unity in Church Order

What will keep unity in the church's order and prevent schism there? Although Scripture uses the word "schism" in a broad sense, yet ecclesiastically it refers to the breach of order in the church. It has often been the case that when the unity of doctrine has been kept, people did not divide from the doctrine but from communion in church ordinances. Now to maintain an entire body in this, consider these rules.

1. Do Not Leave a Church until It Is Impossible to Stay

If the corruption of the church is such that you cannot keep fellowship with her without partaking of her sins, then before you leave that place, take the way the Scripture commands. Be sure that it is not for some lesser corruption, but something which eats up the very vitals of religion. Do not leave it until God leaves it.

Then, before you depart, endeavor (as far as you can) to explain the truth and heal the problem. Plead and strive with the church as if she was your mother. As we have it in Hosea 2:2, "Plead with your mother, plead," because she has committed whoredoms. And then lastly, let your secession be done unwillingly. You are compelled to make this departure because the enemies of all godliness will not tolerate or endure you under their power.

If you have observed these points (leaving only if it is sinful to remain, after endeavors to heal the problem, and then unwillingly), then it is not you who are guilty of any schism or breach, but those who gave the occasion to it. When some of the people of Israel would not join with Jeroboam in his idolatry but separated themselves and went to Jerusalem, where the pure worship was, it was not they who made the schism, but Jeroboam (2 Chron. 11:13–15). So it is with the Reformed churches. The Roman Catholic calls the Protestant a schismatic a thousand times over because he withdraws himself from obedience to the pope as head of the church, but we say that our departure was not a schism but secession. *They* were the schismatics in falling from the original, scriptural order and institutions in the church, insomuch that the pope is the grandest schismatic who ever was in the church. Furthermore, the Reformers did not depart from Rome because of petty corruptions. No, she was a Babylon before they left her, and even then they left her unwillingly. Rome drove the Reformers out, persecuting with fire and faggot.

So we may say, as the reformer Musculus said, that there is a good schism and a bad schism. A good schism is when we divide things that are evilly joined, and a bad schism is when we divide things that are rightly united.

2. Do Not Make Sinful Divisions over Corruptions in Practice

Even if there are many corruptions in church government and administrations, yet you are not to make sinful breaches and rents, for these do more to disturb good people who are weak than to correct the wicked who are proud, as Augustine says. Therefore, there are two things you must do.

First, as far as you can in your calling and position, reprove and oppose the corruptions that abound. The prophets of old, and Christ with His apostles, rebuked with great zeal the corruptions which were prevailing in their times. Although those who are carnal and atheistic, scheming for their own interests, call this schism and faction; yet this is to condemn the generation of all the godly prophets in their times, and to justify Ahab as if not he but Elijah had indeed been the troubler of Israel (1 Kings 18).

Second, when you have done your duty in this way and still corruptions are suffered, leave your complaints with God who has promised at last to take all scandals out of the church. In the meanwhile, patiently sigh and groan under that burden. We should beware of the possibility that we may have a sinful impatience in this situation, as Elijah had to some extent—as well as those disciples who wanted fire immediately to consume the Samaritans because they would not receive Christ.

3. Beware of Your Own Pride

Lastly, to prevent schism in the church's order, take heed of pride, ambition, and seeking great things in the church. It is reported that most of those who made the greatest divisions in the church did it out of discontent when they missed out on honors they had expected. The spirit of Diotrephes, who loved to have the preeminence (3 John 9), has made great divisions. Even the disciples began to quarrel with one another over who should be the chief. This is why our Savior so often urges us to have humility, and enjoins everyone to become like a little child.

Unity in Love

The third way that divisions spoil the unity of the godly is in the way they relate to one another, and that refers to the quarrelling and wrangling which the apostle James speaks against.

Now to prevent these, first remove the cause; kill the serpent in its egg, that is, the lust of the soul. The apostle asks, "From whence come wars and fightings among you? Come they not hence, even of your lusts?" (James 4:1). There is warring within against your own souls first, and then there is warring with one another. Dry up this fountain of lust and then the streams will quickly run no more.

Now any kind of lust unmortified is a spark great enough to set the church on fire. A covetous lust, when people are immoderately given to the world, causes great discord. The Philistines and Isaac strove about the wells, until at last Isaac came to a place which he called Rehoboth, that is, "room" (Gen. 26:22). Here on earth we fall out about earthly things because created things are too scant to give contentment to all, but in heaven there will be room enough. So a proud, envious lust breaks all union within the church to the extent that until coveting is mortified in the heart there will never be union with others. We might mention how this union so excellently prevents the heat of pride, but we have done so already.

Conclusion

Let the sum of all be, as much as in us lies, to put this prayer of Christ into practice. Peace is so great a matter that it is called the peace of God, and God is called the God of peace, and Christ is called our peace, seeing Christ prays for it. We see that it is not all the sermons or all the irenic books that can do any good until God gives one heart. Be importunate therefore with God, and strive with Him for this unspeakable mercy.

CHAPTER 8

The Expansion of Christian Unity

That the world may believe that thou hast sent me.
—John 17:21

This is the consequence and fruit of the unity of believers. When they see such agreement it will convert the world and bring them to the true faith. It is true that Augustine does not make this a consequence but a distinct prayer, as if our Savior's meaning was, "I pray that the world may believe in me." Although there may be some truth in this, I think that the context is to the contrary. It is plain that the word "that" or "so that" denotes here some consequence that flows from the unity of believers.

Others do not understand faith here as saving but rather as historical faith. By "the world" they understand reprobates, since even these can by the preaching of the Word and other demonstrations be convinced to believe Christian doctrine. Thus they say that Christ does not pray for the world of reprobates here but only as a consequence of believers among themselves.

But (together with Calvin) I rather take "the world" here for mankind, in a negative and indefinite sense— *negative*, as referring to those who do not yet believe, and *indefinite*, referring to those who do believe. Some truly and savingly believe; others have something that looks like faith but for only a season. We can summarize what he is saying like this: Christ prays that believers may be united among themselves because this opens a wide opportunity for the progress of the gospel. By this unity the world may be persuaded that Christ is indeed the true Messiah because He has brought such true peace among His disciples.

Unity among believers is a special means of enlarging the kingdom of Christ. Nothing gives quite so much obstruction to the gospel, and scandal to the world (keeping it away from faith in Christ), as seeing those who profess Christ divided and subdivided into many sects and opinions. It is innate to everybody to think that truth cannot be contrary to itself, that Christ cannot be divided, and that the Spirit of God is the same Spirit. Therefore it is superficially very plausible to conclude that certainly these people are not of Christ and do not have His Spirit, because they are so contrary to one another.

No wonder, therefore, if Christ earnestly prays for unity among believers as being the most effectual means to propagate and preserve the gospel. This made the apostle—when he had spent the chapter chiefly saluting the saints (an expression of dear love)—most fervently break out, saying, "I beseech you, brethren, mark them which cause divisions and offences...and avoid them" (Rom. 16:17). We are in a special manner to take heed of such turbulent and divisive persons. The apostle gives this as a general characteristic of all who do not serve Jesus Christ but instead serve their own lusts and ends.

Only the Right Kind of Unity
Answers Christ's Prayer

Even though the doctrine states that unity among believers is a means of enlarging Christ's kingdom, yet unity alone is not an infallible mark of the true church. And though our Savior insists on the unity of believers as a sign of His disciples and a means of winning others to the faith, yet unity simply as such is not an inseparable note of the true church. Roman Catholics maintain that where we see a church in its members all united together, and united under one visible head and pastor, there we are to conclude is the true church. And on the contrary, when we see divisions and multiplicities of sects and opinions, there cannot be any true church. Indeed they have no more convenient way to entangle people and to fill people's hearts with prejudices against the truth than pointing out the many opinions that are among us.

But to this we answer these things.

The Right Kind of Unity Includes True Doctrine

First, unity without true doctrine cannot be any distinctive note of a true church. A whole church may be universally corrupted so that neither the worship nor the truths of God are received in any visible way, and yet in this universal corruption they are all united as one. Jews and Muslims have great unity among themselves, yet who will conclude that the truth is among them? It is necessary, therefore, that to organizational unity there must be joined true and sound doctrine.

In the second place, we say there is no real reason for Roman Catholics to claim that they have unity among themselves, for they do not only fight against Protestants but even with one another. Witness the Jesuits against the Dominicans, including in points of serious controversy, and it is also the same between Thomists and Scotists. Now to this the Roman Catholic apologist Cardinal Robert Bellarmine (1542–1621), provides these answers.

First, he says that the differences between groups within the Roman Catholic Church are not in substantial things; they are only in secondary points. But this is only the same as what we say, that is, that Protestants (who are truly Protestant) agree in fundamentals. So that although there are great disputes in things to do with the faith, yet they do not disagree about the foundation itself. Additionally, within the Roman Catholic Church they have in fact disagreed over fundamentals. For example, it is a principle of religion with them that the pope is above the council, and yet there have been hot differences among them on this point, with some asserting that the pope may be deposed by the council and reputed as a heretic. Certainly with them, either the pope or a council is the general head of the church (and according to them it is necessary for salvation to be in obedience to this head), yet they cannot agree who the head is.

Second, Bellarmine says, if the Roman Catholic Church has any divisions, they arise from the mere malice of the devil, not for lack of a remedy to keep the unity. For they have a visible judge to determine all controversies, whereas (according to him) the differences among Protestants arise from their doctrine itself because they acknowledge no visible efficacious remedy to such contentions. But this also is answered easily. All the differences among the people of God come from both the devil without and corruptions within. The devil is not wholly conquered, nor are our corruptions altogether vanquished, and therefore it cannot but be that breaches and wounds will sometimes be made.

Yet, the Reformed have a more sure and efficacious remedy than they have for resolving all differences. They indeed claim that the pope or a council is a visible judge to end all controversies, but these being men are subject to ignorance and passions and so cannot perform the office of an infallible visible judge; they are not sufficiently qualified for this role. And they have not in fact silenced all those debates that are among them. Some of these disputes are as fervent as ever. Neither has the pope yet intervened to decide whether those doctrines about "middle knowledge" and absolute predefinitions and the controversies that depend on them are true on the Dominicans' side, or their adversaries'.

Therefore thirdly, we hold the Scriptures to be the infallible and unerring rule, and therefore we claim to have a proper and sufficient means to end all controversies. It may be said that many differences arise about the sense of the Scripture, and that therefore it cannot be a judge, but instead the church must be. However, we reply that many controversies also may arise about the church itself, the authority of it, and its infallibility, and therefore they who acknowledge the Scripture as the only adequate rule of faith do thereby confess a powerful remedy to remove all differences.

The Right Kind of Unity May Be Opposed by Satan

Visible unity is not in fact always a note of the church. This is apparent from the opposition of Satan against the church's peace and quietness. In matters of practice, peace and quietness are not always a sign of a good conscience, for our Savior says the devil—like a strong man who safely guards his goods—keeps all things quiet while he rules (Luke 11:21). So it is also in respect of churches. Many times a false, superstitious church has more prosperity and ease than a true one because the devil will not disturb his own. But where the kingdom of Christ is, there the devil desires to erect his throne also. When the good seed was sown, the devil sowed his tares on top. In a wilderness or a place of weeds, he would not have been so diligent. Therefore, breaches and divisions, because they are a kind or part of afflictions and troubles, may be more likely to accompany the true church than outward unity and prosperity.

The Right Kind of Unity May Be Imperfect for the Time Being

We grant that if the church of God were fully perfected, both in respect of knowledge and holiness, it would always have unity. We see this in heaven where the church is perfect and there is no difference at all. But because we know only in part, and we are godly only in part, therefore these breaches may be made upon us. There may then be discord and division in an imperfect church, but not in a perfect church. Therefore our Savior's prayer will have its ultimate accomplishment only in heaven.

Why Is Unity an Attractive Magnet to Draw Others to the Faith?

Let us now proceed to show why unity is such an attractive and a divine magnet to bring others to the faith.

1. First, unity is attractive because people instinctively cleave to a way of religion that will abide and continue. "Hath a nation changed their gods?" asks the prophet (Jer. 2:11). The statesman Gamaliel argued that they should not oppose the Christians, for if that religion were of God, it would stand (Acts 5:39).

It is a clear axiom, confirmed also by our Savior, that no kingdom divided against itself can stand (Luke 11:17). By that argument our Savior proves that He could not cast out devils by the help of the devils, for then the devil would overthrow his own kingdom. Divisions, then, and differences are of necessity a stumbling block, for who would go into a house which has its walls falling away from one another? Who would venture into a ship which is full of leaks? Does not everyone say, "Leave them alone, they will destroy one another; they need no outward force to ruin them, they will consume themselves sooner or later"?

2. Second, unity is attractive because everyone acknowledges that God is a God of peace and of order. The apostle uses this consideration to restrain the confusions and disorderly customs which the Christians had in their public assemblies (1 Cor. 14). If then God were a God of peace and order, how can anyone think His truth and people are marked by disorder and confusion? It was in building Babel, and not Jerusalem, that they were so confounded that they did not understand each

other's language. Where envying and strife is, there is confusion and every evil work (James 3:16). Now everyone is apt to argue—certainly if this was the way of God—if these were the people of God, there would not be such confusion among them. The God who made this great world in such excellent order would much more make His church, His choicest plant, more beautiful.

3. Third, unity is attractive because anyone who has heard of the Holy Ghost—that He alone leads into all truth—will quickly conclude that this Spirit cannot be against Himself. And this is the more observable because every group claims to have the Spirit of God, which is why John commands us to test the spirits and not to believe every spirit, that is, every doctrine claimed to be of the Spirit (1 John 4:1). If then everyone pleads God's Spirit and His teaching, people are all the more confirmed in their unbelief when they see the church holding to contrary spirits of contrary doctrines condemning each other with great zeal.

What a world of hurt divisions among the godly do! It is a wonderful work of God that any are brought off from their former vain habits when the spirit of division has so sadly reigned among us. No wonder that conversion is so rare a thing, and so few come in cordially to confess Christ, seeing that such sad offences are made by these differences between the godly. And those who cause them actively stand in the way of souls gaining heaven!

The Sins Bred by Disunity in the World among the Godly

In the next place, let us consider briefly what sins the divisions among the godly tend to breed in the world.

The first is atheism and irreligion, and the persuasion that there is no such thing as a true religion, but that all religions are the fancies and imaginations of men. No doubt but thousands are confirmed in their atheistic way. They believe there is no God at all and no religion is better than another, for they see that scarcely anyone can agree about it.

The second is stiffness and obstinacy in their erroneous and superstitious ways. No doubt our disunity keeps multitudes hardened in their pre-Reformation ways. And why? Because there are so many ways, and everyone has a religion for himself; therefore they decide to stay where they are, although they do not know where they may stumble to at last. They think to abandon their old ways is to abandon their old wits at the same time.

The third is fickleness, inconstancy, and skepticism. There are many in our day called Seekers, who think there is now no church since the apostles' times, and therefore they are in their souls what Cain was in his body, vagabonds in the earth (Gen. 4:12). And where has all this come from? The bitter root is diversity of opinions, which they entertain one after another, and which at last makes them quite without any foundation at all.

Application
Beware of Causing Division

To every Christian again and again I say, take heed of causing divisions in the church of God. Be afraid to make any unnecessary rent by any opinion or practice, for when you do, you are doing as much as lies in you to hinder others from coming to the kingdom of heaven. Will this not be a sad aggravation of your sin, when men damned in hell shall plead, "Lord, I was coming, even I was hopefully inclining to the things of Christianity, but this man and that man by their divisiveness stopped me!" Or, "He made me a proselyte to some pernicious way while I was going to Christ. If this man had not been in the way, I would never have been seduced." Certainly, if our Savior pronounces a woe to those by whom offences come, how sore will it fall on those who make these offences in the highest degree?

Beware of Divisions Becoming a Spiritual Snare

Take heed that these divisions do not prove a snare to you. Bewail times of division, but make sure they do not divide between you and God, or you and truth. Instead:

1. Walk humbly, renouncing your own strength, for it is God, not yourself, who must preserve you.

2. Pray much for the Spirit of God to give you His anointing—and senses exercised to discern between good and evil.

3. Take heed of fomenting differences and making the wounds wider. Instead, like the good Samaritan, bring oil, not salt, to the wounds.

4. Lastly, let this make you long for heaven, where the strife between brethren will cease.

CHAPTER 9

The Value of Christian Unity

That they may be one, even as we are one.
—John 17:22

Unity among Christians is part of the glory which Christ has purchased for them. Christ gives the glory He received from the Father to those who believe in Him, that they may be one. Now the word "that" or "so that" here, as in other places, may be taken either as the end or goal of this glory, or as specifying a part of the glory which He gives to them. Some understand it as describing and determining what it is He would give them, that is, the glory of unity and agreement. As Chrysostom observes, this was more admirable than the signs and doctrine in which they abounded. Their unity glorified them more than their miracles. Others understand it as the end and fruit of the glory they received, that is, all the heavenly benefits and privileges granted to them.

I make the observation from these two interpretations, and from the context of the words, that unity among believers is part of the glory which Christ as Mediator has obtained for them.

In this doctrinal proposition we should take note of three things in particular.

1. Unity among believers is part of the spiritual glory which Christ purchased for them.

2. Christ as Mediator purchased unity as well as other privileges.

3. Believers cannot have unity except from Christ. Till He commands these dry bones to come together and be united, they lie scattered up and down.

Unity Is Part of the Church's Glory

This unity is both actively and passively part of the church's glory. *Actively*, they may in a humble and holy manner rejoice in it. Not like those who confidently and falsely triumph in the unity of the papacy, but in a godly and sober manner. For if schisms and divisions in the church did so greatly divide and rend Paul's heart, no doubt but their unity and harmony did as much make him rejoice. This is why he speaks so emphatically, "If there be therefore any consolation in Christ, if any comfort of love, if any fellowship of the Spirit, if any bowels and mercies, fulfil ye my joy, that ye be likeminded"

(Phil. 2:1–2). It is then the minister's glory and the church's glory to walk in lovely harmony. This occurs when in the church, as in Solomon's temple, the sound of the hammer is not heard, or when (as God promised in respect of temporal peace, the sword should be turned into ploughshares) the controversial and polemical part of theology shall be changed into the practical and affectionate part.

Unity is also part of the glory of the church *passively*, in the sense that for it we are exceedingly to glorify and praise God. We should see the spiritual peace of the church as a greater mercy than all external mercies. What a burdensome thing is it when Jerusalem is made a Babel, when the church is like the chaos and confusion that was made at first, when God brings the kind of judgment on the church (as at one time He brought a temporal one on her enemies) where every man's weapon is against his neighbor, until they have destroyed one another. When therefore we see God forming the hearts of believers to value unity, we ought to praise God for it, as being a special means of promoting Christ's kingdom.

Why Is It the Glory of Believers to Be at Unity?

1. It is the glory of believers because this unity will exalt them in the very hearts and thoughts of their greatest enemies. What is glory but being well known, the famous acknowledging of the excellency of a thing? Now nothing will sooner divulge the fame of the church, and

make the noise of it to go through the land, than unity and agreement. As Solomon's wisdom spread itself over the world, to the extent that many came from afar to see and admire it, so it will be also for the harmony of the church. This is why the psalmist put a "Behold!" on it. "Behold, how good and how pleasant it is for brethren to dwell together in unity!" (Ps. 133:1). You have heard how the heathen admired the love of the early Christians, declaring how believers loved one another and called each other brothers! Whereas now they might say, "Behold how they hate and oppose one another, calling one another by all uncharitable names!" It is unity then that makes the church's fame go throughout the world.

2. It is the glory of believers because glory arises from the exquisite beauty of the church's unity. The beauty of a thing is the glory of it, and beauty arises from the sweet harmony and proportion of all the parts. This is the unity of the church, when every member of it is harmoniously joined to the other, and when there is no dissonance or difference. Certainly, it is a better wish to see the church in this glory than Augustine's wish to see Rome in all her temporal glory. If any member is deformed, or out of proportion with the other parts, it makes a body unlovely and uncomely. So it is here that if anyone makes a split, is proud, forward, or contrary, the glory of the church is departed.

3. It is the glory of believers because the happiness and blessedness of those in a church is in their communal, shared graces. A church denotes some society and company. Now the advantage of their graces comes by their union: if one part of the body were divided from the other, no mutual help could be supplied. The reason for nerves and ligaments in the body is to unite each part to another. If there is no union in a civil society, its glory presently dies. Divisions, like moths, rise from within, and do immediately consume. If then the happiness of believers lies in their communal graces and duties, what can be more glorious than unity, which is the only means of procuring subservience to one another! If several cities are supplied by pipes of water to one another, and those pipes are stopped or cut, it necessarily brings destruction.

Christ the Mediator Purchased the Privilege of Unity

Christ not only died to justify and sanctify His people but also to unite them. This should teach us several things.

Divisions Are Not a Light Matter

It should not be accounted a slight and little sin to make any breaches or divisions in God's church, to do anything through strife and vainglory. Why? Because Christ died to oppose this. As Mediator, He intended not only to save His people but also to bring them into one. Why then do you by your contentions or by your heretical opinions sin in this way against Christ's death? His intercession and His prayer are for the same effects. You see in this chapter that His prayer for unity is reiterated over and over again. Christ had this in His thoughts even in His very death.

It was also at His death that He appointed the sacrament of the Lord's Supper. Although this sacrament is chiefly to seal God's grace to us, yet it also signifies the love we ought to have toward one another. The apostle argues that as the several grains make up one bread, so do the godly make up one mystical body (1 Corinthians 10). Divisions in the church are therefore against Christ's death, and against the sacrament of His death. Shall we therefore run into sins that have such a heinous aggravation?

Christ's People Should Long for Unity

The people of God, where they see these divisions, are to make a good use of this argument for unity. When they groan under any corruption and would like to have mastery over it, they run to the blood of Christ, praying, "O Lord, did not Christ die so that these sins would die? Was not Christ crucified to crucify these lusts?" So it ought to be in the matter of unity: "O Lord, make all Thy people of one heart, of one mind and spirit, because Christ died for this also. Let not His death be in vain. Thou wouldst not suffer His bones to be broken, nor His garment divided, why then shall His church be torn and divided?" Do not think that human policies and invented schemes of syncretism will be able to solder the church together. It must be the blood of Christ that obtains this.

Christ Sets the Pattern for Our Unity

Christ did not only meritoriously purchase this unity by His death but in Him exemplarily and formally we are made one, so that Christ is both the moral cause of this unity and the example also. By being both God and man in one person, He made God and man one. When there was such an infinite distance before, there is made the most intimate union that can be, even a hypostatical union between God and man.

Now though we cannot attain to this kind of union, yet it is by reason of this union that all believers are made one with God, and one among themselves. Hence there are frequent expressions of our being "in Him," of being "engrafted into Him," of "living in Him," all of which denote our intimate union with Him. As Christ is not divided in Himself (it is not that the divine nature wills one thing and the human nature the contrary, but they have the same will), so it ought to be with us. One believer should not judge one thing and another the contrary; one love one thing and another the contrary. But as Christ and the Father were one, so believers ought to be one.

Christ Alone Can Create Unity

God in Christ is the only cause of unity among believers. Christ as Mediator procures it, and God through His merits vouchsafes it. This includes the following two things.

Only God Can Subdue Our Sinful Corruptions

Such is the corruption of every one, regenerate and unregenerate, that they would no more unite than grains of sand would if God did not bring it about. Take people by nature and they are wolves and devils to one another, to the extent that the preserving of commonwealths and civil societies is sometimes used as a demonstration of the existence of God. For if you consider what people are by nature, it is a wonder that the whole world is not full of Cains, and a mere Aceldama—a "field of blood" (Acts 1:19).

God, who keeps the sea within its bounds so that it does not overflow, also restrains and chains up human corruptions so that everything is not in confusion. Although corruption is subdued in a great measure in the regenerate, yet that is not like the root of the tree in Nebuchadnezzar's dream, which had a chain on it so that it would never grow. For this tree of corruption would be continually sprouting out in strife and contentions if God did not put bounds to it. Not only secular histories but also ecclesiastical histories abundantly witness that divisions and differences have been the ruin of most churches. Truly we may apply Job's saying to the church, "When he giveth quietness, who then can make trouble? and when he hideth his face, who then can behold him?" (Job 34:29). It is in the nature even of godly people to be so many Phaetons setting the church on fire, if God by mercy did not prevent it.[1]

Only God Can Reverse the Judgment of Disunity

It is only through Christ that God procures spiritual concord because it is through Christ that God is pleased with His church and reconciled. Now it is God's anger for sin that turns churches and states upside down; even as you see the tempestuous winds fill the sea with waves and unquietness. If God is at peace, all is at peace. When God was angry with Abimelech, He sent an evil spirit between him and the men of Shechem (Judg. 9:23), and this, like a fire, consumed them. So when Solomon had displeased God by his idolatries, God stirred up Solomon's adversary against him and eventually divided the kingdom.

So you see, it is God's anger for sin that makes discord and implacable contentions break forth in society. And so it is also in the church. When God is angry, He allows heretics and schismatics to arise, who divide the church into as many pieces as the Levite's wife was. Till

---

1. In Greek mythology, Phaeton set the earth on fire and was himself destroyed by a thunderbolt.

God's anger is pacified, there can never be any settling or uniting. Instead, it is like two passengers in a ship at deadly feud with one another, earnestly looking to see which would be drowned first, and not at all endeavoring to save the ship. So private jealousies have undone the public good. The heathen may rise up against the church of God to condemn us, for before the Romans entered into the Senate house to consult about the public good, they first went and worshiped in a temple dedicated to Jupiter called a depository because they deposited their enmities there. But we go to prayer, to sacraments, and offer our gift at the altar, though we remember that people justly have many things against us.

Application

Is peace and unity among the godly their glory? Did Christ die for it? Is it only God who gives it? Then under all our breaches and differences, let us apply ourselves to Him who has this sovereign power over people's hearts. It just needs Him to speak and the winds and the waves will presently cease. He can quickly remove the bitter spirit of contradiction and cause everyone to be of one mind. Certainly our sins have highly displeased God, so that He still allows His church to wallow in her own blood, with her wounds not yet healed.

CHAPTER 10

The Perfection of Christian Unity

Christ prayed, "That they may be made perfect in one" (John 17:23). These words contain the effect and fruit of the unity mentioned previously; that is, where Christ is in us, and the Father in Him. Our Savior speaks of a threefold unity here: (a) of the Father with Christ, as Mediator; (b) of Christ, as Mediator and Head, with His church; and (c) of believers among themselves. The unity of Christ with believers, as He is their Head, is the cause of their union and communion with one another.

This is the last time our Savior mentions this matter of unity. In this prayer for believers our Savior prays four times for unity. This demonstrates an exceedingly ardent love and desire for it. Every expression seems to rise higher than the previous: (a) that they may be one; (b) that they may be one in us; (c) that they may be one, even as we are one; (d) that they may be made perfect in one.

The original Greek words that are best translated as finish, complete, or fulfill can be used to denote consummating something with perfection. Sometimes these words are used in relation to setting apart and consecrating things (Heb. 2:10; 5:9; 7:28). It is true that all believers are consecrated and set apart as holy from the world to God, but it is their perfect consummation in unity that is primarily intended here. Although this will not be complete until heaven, it is begun in this life.

How Are They Perfect in One?
Sincerity
Being made perfect in one implies sincerity and uprightness. Christian unity must be from a pure heart and an unfeigned faith. The word "perfect" is often used in contrast to that which is false and counterfeit. Many are said to walk with a perfect heart because they did not walk with "a heart and a heart," by dissimulation.[1] It means a perfection of essence and parts, not a perfection of degrees.

This indeed is greatly to be urged, that as all the other things in the godly are sincere, so should their unity be sincere. They should be joined together from spiritual principles and by spiritual means. It was the position

---

1. The Hebrew phrase "a heart and a heart" (meaning "a double heart") is used in passages of Scripture that speak of hypocrisy (see Ps. 12:2 and 1 Chron. 12:33, for example).

of Roman philosophers that friendship could only be among the good, and that whatever friendship came only from convenience or pleasure, and not from virtue, did not deserve the name of friendship. How much more is this true in unity among the godly, which has for its cause and origin Christ Himself, and for its pattern the unity that the Father and Son have? To be perfect in unity, then, is to have sincere hearts toward one another. As the apostle says, "Let love be without dissimulation" (Rom. 12:9). Let there be no water to debase this wine; let not this beautiful fruit be rotten at the core.

Integrity

Secondly, to be perfect in unity implies not only sincerity but also the integrity of all the substantial and essential matters in which this oneness consists.

You have heard that the unity of believers flows in two great streams: one of faith, in respect of doctrine, and the other of charity, in respect of life and affections. Therefore, if either of these is lacking, the unity is dissolved. If we claim to have love but yet there is no divine truth, this is conspiracy, not unity. And if we claim to have faith but we do not love, we do not yet have the mark of the true disciples of Christ. Let the church of God, then, make sure that it has these two pillars, like Jachin and Boaz, to bear it up (1 Kings 7:21). All unity without truth is like a stately building on sand, and truth without love is like a foundation without superstructure. Pray therefore that the Spirit of God would lead the church into all truth for the former, and would work those sanctifying fruits of it, including love, peace, and meekness, for the latter.

Progress

Thirdly, the phrase "perfect in one" implies an increase and daily progress in the way of unity.

For though the church of Christ is His body, yet it is a growing body. It has not come to its full stature and indeed it will not in this life. Yet there are further degrees to be attained. We are to grow to a perfect man in Christ Jesus (Eph. 4:13), and we read of many who are called perfect, as in 1 Corinthians 2:6 and Hebrews 5:14—not in an absolute sense but comparatively, because they are carried on to further degrees of grace than others. We are not then to think that any church will have such a perfect unity in this life that it is not capable of being more perfected. In even the best-constituted churches there are several imperfections, there is much weakness, there are many carnal affections, which are apt to discompose the beautiful frame of the church.

Use of Means

Fourthly, to be "perfect in one" implies that believers are perfected in the means which are appointed by God for this unity. Since perfected means are necessary to completely achieve the end, the end can never be better enjoined than by exhorting to make a good use of the means. So if the church of God is to be more perfected in one, it must more faithfully improve the means of unity. There are two special means of making progress in unity.

First is the preaching of the Word of God. Just as preaching is necessary for the church to be called out of the world, so also preaching is necessary to keep it in purity and unity. The Word of God preached is the only means appointed to remove ignorance and mortify corruptions, which are the tares that hinder the good seed. As the envious man sows these, so the Spirit of Christ by the Word works the exact opposite. Hence, the ministry is appointed as a means to bring us to this perfect stature (Eph. 4:13). Far be it therefore from preachers to make divisions and rents in the church of God when their main role and work is to proclaim peace. The good shepherd will not permit his sheep to fight with one another to be destroyed.

Second, the sacrament of the Lord's Supper is a special means of preserving unity, and indeed of perfecting it. The apostle speaks fully to this: "For we being many are one bread, and one body: for we are all partakers of that one bread" (1 Cor. 10:17). For that matter, one baptism is presented as a reason and obligation to be united (Eph. 4:1–6). Therefore, the more graciously and perfectly these ordinances are received, the more this unity is confirmed and established. That is why the early Christians, who had one soul and one heart, were also constant in their breaking of bread, by which their mutual love was strongly preserved.

Bellarmine, although he was a Roman Catholic theologian, makes a good point when he speaks of six kinds of unity in the church.

The first is in respect of the God who calls, although, as he says, this makes the church not so much one as *under one*. The second is in respect of the ultimate goal, the salvation to which the church is called, which makes the church not so much one, as *toward one*. The third is in respect of the means of faith and sacraments, which makes the church not so much one as *by one*. The fourth is in respect of the Holy Spirit, who steers like a captain outside of the ship, which makes the church not so much one as *under one*. The fifth is in respect of Christ, as an internal and conjoined head. And the sixth is in respect of the connection of the members among themselves. In these two last respects it is properly *one*—one body, one people, and one society.

Eternity

Fifthly, they will be "perfect in one" in eternity. This unity will be wholly perfected in heaven. Then all partition walls will be destroyed; then it shall no more be said, "I am of Paul, and I am of Apollos," but God will be all in all. As this life is a place like Hadadrimmon, a valley of tears (Zech. 12:11), for bewailing the corruptions and sins among us, so it is a place for mourning the divisions and breaches that are upon us. But in heaven, all different opinions and all different ways will cease. Therefore, although this unity may be attained in principle in this life, yet in the life to come it will be totally completed. Here it is perfect in principle, in the sense that the endeavors and aspirations of the godly are to have perfection in the church in grace, just as it shall be with the church hereafter in glory. Certainly, if it were not accomplished in heaven, then it would not be the case that all tears would be wiped away, nor would the reproach of Jerusalem cease.

Why Are They Perfect in One?

Now let us consider what is the cause of their being "perfect in one." It is because Christ is in them. The cause is no human strength or outward wisdom and policy, but Christ Himself giving us a lively communication of grace to enable us to be perfect in one.

The divisions and breaches of the godly, like the divisions of Reuben, have made sad workings of heart (Judg. 5:15–16), and many have come running in with water to quench this fire. Some argue that the only means of preserving unity is to acknowledge one visible head in the church (such as the pope), yet experience shows the inadequacy of this. Several antidotes have been prescribed against this corruption of disunity, but when all is done, it is only the power of Jesus Christ, as Head of His church, that works this sweet harmony.

It is true indeed that many rules and means of peace-keeping are commended by wise and godly men to make unity, but these work only by moral persuasion. What really brings it about is the Lord Christ Himself, as the fountain of this unity—because this unity among believers is not only external but also internal and spiritual. No man can work this unity in the hearts of the godly any more than he can work purity and holiness. Therefore we see in the text that it is because Christ is in us, and the Father in Christ, that the godly are perfected in one. It requires a divine, supernatural power to bring the godly into heavenly harmony, even as it requires divine power to make them godly in the first place.

The cause of the perfect and consummate unity which believers ought to have is *the Father and Christ being in them*. There could be no union in the body if the Head did not unite it. All union that believers experience flows from Christ first as their Head and Mediator. Whatever unity they may have which does not first rise from this spring is merely human and of the flesh. Hence, in this prayer Christ commends it to God to work it, as being beyond all human power to effect it.

Christ in Them Causes Spiritual Unity

Christ being in the believer is a cause of the unity itself. For as we have said, this unity, though external, yet is chiefly spiritual and internal. That is, the harmonious knitting and joining of all the members of Christ together, in Him their head.

Now as this is wholly spiritual, none can produce it but God alone, for naturally we are disjoined from God and full of opposition to Him. Therefore to be made a member of Christ, and implanted into Him, cannot be by any other but the Spirit of God. Those dry bones in Ezekiel could not gather together of their own accord, nor can a twig, a scion, graft itself into a stock. So it is here. Till the Spirit of God joins us to Christ, we are enemies and adversaries to Him. Therefore, the power which gives grace is the only power which unites. As in the natural body, the same cause which makes a member makes it also a united member.

Therefore, in all the factions and divisions we see among the godly, we ought to have our eyes up more to God, to consider that it is the same power which makes them holy which must unite them. Indeed to make them gracious and holy in the first place is the greater work. Unity would flow as a necessary result of our membership in Christ, except for the fact that our corruptions are still too strong and apt to disturb all.

Christ in Them Causes Proportionate Unity

Christ's being in us is not only the cause of our unity but also of the harmonious suitable proportion we have to each other. There is an admirable description of this harmonious suitableness in the unity of Christ's body in

Colossians 2:19: "the Head, from which all the body by joints and bands having nourishment ministered, and knit together, increaseth with the increase of God."

This text is full of rich and glorious matter. The apostle is saying that the reason false teachers promoted the worship of angels, introduced human traditions, and effectively set up other means and ways of justification is that they did not hold fast to the Head. Every Christian in all spiritual concernments is still to look up to Christ as the Head, and not to let Him go.

This comes from a twofold, precious effect of this Head. The first effect is the union of believers to Christ. As the body receives nourishment by its joints and ligaments and sinews, so every Christian has nourishment from Christ. Now the joint that supplies these spiritual helps is chiefly the Spirit of God. "If any man have not the Spirit of Christ, he is none of his" (Rom. 8:9). As a member is not truly united to the head unless it has the same form as the head, so neither is somebody really united to Christ if they lack the Spirit of Christ (see Col. 2:19). The Spirit of Christ is here said to administer nourishment. This was originally a reference to supplying the ornaments which were necessary by those who held sacred dances and festivities, but here it signifies the supply of the things that are necessary for spiritual purposes, and it is referred to as a full, plentiful, and abundant supply. So that you see it is Christ's Spirit, not ours, which enables us.

The second benefit flowing from Christ our Head belongs to the members themselves. They are knit together. The bands or ligaments which knit them together are again chiefly the Spirit of God, though gifts and graces do also ordinarily unite. As the apostle says, we all "by one Spirit are…baptized into one body." (1 Cor. 12:13) The Spirit of God, who is in Christ, also works in all believers, inflaming them and stirring them up to the graces by which they have intimate communion with one another.

Now from these two benefits we have the admirable fruit that the body grows with the increase of God. The spiritual growth of Christians is called "the increase of God," partly because only God is the cause and producer of it, partly because the nature of this increase is divine and heavenly, and partly because it is for the glory and honor of God.

So by all this we see that every true member of Christ is a thriving and growing member—one who grows harmoniously according to their respective nature—and all this comes wholly by the Spirit of Christ. Unity in its harmonious increase depends solely on Him (see Eph. 4:15–16).

Christ in Them Causes Lasting Unity

Christ's being in us is the cause of the perpetuity and constancy of the unity the godly have. This union in Christ's body can never be dissolved. As the personal union of Christ's human and divine natures could never be divided, so neither can the mystical union between Christ and His people ever be divided. Therefore, theologians are right to use Christ's indwelling in us as a reason to assert the perseverance of the saints.

Application

Why is it that even among the godly there are so many differences of opinion and burnings of heart? It is because Christ is not in them in such a powerful and efficacious manner as He might be. The dark night and misty fogs can no more endure before the glorious beams of the sun than corrupt passions and contentions can stand before the Sun of Righteousness, when risen to its vertical point. Under the equatorial sun, there cannot be any cold frosts, so neither under the efficacious presence of Christ can there be such sinful breaches.